Easy Peasy
Language Arts 7
Lesson Guide

D1247354

Copyright 2019 Lee Giles
All rights reserved.
ISBN- 9781794677241

Cover Design: Stephen Rutherford

Welcome to the EP Language Arts 7 Lesson Guide!

This book teaches the lessons you'll need to complete the Language Arts 7 Workbook. It was written for the student. You should read the lesson each lesson and then follow the directions on the worksheet for that lesson in your workbook.

The answers for the workbook are in the back of this book. Complete your worksheet before checking your answers. Learn from your mistakes. Mistakes are learning opportunities. Don't waste your opportunities! If you cheat and just copy answers, you are only cheating yourself. The point is to learn and to educate yourself. Education is power. Cheating is lazy. Lazy people aren't powerful!

This course covers all language arts topics including: writing, grammar, and spelling. Throughout the year students will be writing non-fiction and descriptive essays, and the year ends with writing a novel.

If you get to the end of a page, turn the page to see if there is more to your lesson!

Have a great year!

Note: We used to call each lesson a day: "Day 1," "Day 2," etc. We've replaced those days with "lessons," but you'll see "day" still in the mini pages in the answer section. Those pages are the same, not outdated, just that one word is changed.

Lesson 1
1. Today's assignment is to write a motto for the school year. Inspire yourself to be dedicated to doing your best and having a great attitude. Use this year as a step to your future, because it is!
   - Imbue gratefulness
   - Pay attention to the quintessential
   - Start a ripple
2. Here are some more words if you need more inspirations: dulcet, ebullience, imbue, panacea.
3. Hang your motto up near your workspace. Live up to it.

Lesson 2
Writing
1. Look for rhyming words in this poem, *Hope Is a Thing with Feathers* by Emily Dickinson. There is rhyming but it isn't a strict rhyme.
   - "Hope" is the thing with feathers
     That perches in the soul
     And sings the tune without the words
     And never stops at all,
     And sweetest in the gale is heard;
     And sore must be the storm
     That could abash the little bird
     That kept so many warm.
     I've heard it in the chillest land
     And on the strangest sea,
     Yet never, in extremity,
     It asked a crumb of me.
2. Look for rhythm in the poem. (Count syllables.) There is rhythm, but again, it isn't a strict pattern.
3. Choose a feeling to write a poem about.
4. Think of an image to describe it, like the bird in the poem describes hope.
5. Write a poem in the style of this poem. Use her rhyme and rhythm patterns.

Lesson 3
Writing
1. On your workbook page is the poem, *A Thanksgiving to God, for his House.* Look for its rhythm and rhyming patterns.
2. Choose a point you want to make.
3. Make it! Write a poem in the same style.

Lesson 4
Writing
1. Write a psalm.
   - Here are the first two verses of Psalm 150.
     Praise ye the Lord. Praise God in his sanctuary: praise him in the firmament of his power.

Praise him for his mighty acts: praise him according to his excellent greatness.
2. Use at least one simile. Need a reminder? A simile compares two unlike things using the words like or as.

Lesson 5
Writing
1. Tell a story in couplets. Your story can be as simple as waking up and eating breakfast, but you have to write at least two couplets.
2. What's a couplet? A couplet is a pair of rhyming lines of same length. Here is an example from a Keat's poem:
   • Of the forest's whispering fleeces, Since men knew nor rent nor leases.
3. Two couplets is four lines. That's the minimum.

Lesson 6
Spelling
1. Have someone read your spelling words from the Lesson 6 answer page in the back of the Lesson Guide. Write them as best as you can.
2. Check them and write correctly any that were misspelled.
3. Figure out why you wrote what you did and how you can remember the correct way, maybe by pronouncing the word a little differently.
4. Then try writing those corrected words again without looking.

Lesson 7
Spelling
1. Work on your spelling.
2. This unscramble uses the words from Lesson 6, so you can peek back if necessary.
3. The point is to pay attention to how they are spelled.
4. When your work is checked, make sure the spelling of each word is checked.
5. Rewrite any that were spelled wrong; don't only fix them.

Lesson 8
Spelling
1. Fill in the blanks.
2. Again, these are the same spelling words as Lesson 6 and 7, so you can look back for a hint IF you can't figure out a word.
3. When your work is checked, make sure the spelling of each word is checked.
4. Rewrite any that were spelled wrong; don't only fix them.

Lesson 9
Spelling
1. Play hangman. Have someone play with you.
   • They will find the word to use for Lesson 9 in the answer key.
   • They will tell you how many letters are in the word. Draw that number of blanks on a piece of paper.
   • Guess one letter at a time. If the letter is in the word, have them tell you which blank or blanks it goes in. Write it in.

- If you want, for each wrong guess, draw a piece of a picture. Try to guess the word before you finish your picture.
2. This one should be done without looking back!

Lesson 10
Spelling
1. Take the spelling test. Have someone read the words to you from the answers for Lesson 10. Have them read each word, one at a time, while you write it down.
2. Any word you spell incorrectly today, rewrite five times, correctly of course.

Lesson 11
Spelling
5. Have someone read your spelling words from the Lesson 11 answer page in the back of the Lesson Guide. Write them as best as you can.
6. Check them and write correctly any that were misspelled.
7. Figure out why you wrote what you did and how you can remember the correct way, maybe by pronouncing the word a little differently.
8. Then try writing those corrected words again without looking.

Lesson 12
Spelling
1. Work on your spelling.
2. This unscramble uses the words from Lesson 11, so you can peek back if necessary.
3. The point is to pay attention to how they are spelled.
4. When your work is checked, make sure the spelling of each word is checked.
5. Rewrite any that were spelled wrong; don't only fix them.

Lesson 13
Spelling
1. Fill in the blanks.
2. Again, these are the same spelling words from Lesson 11, so you can look back for a hint IF you can't figure out a word.
3. When your work is checked, make sure the spelling of each word is checked.
4. Rewrite any that were spelled wrong; don't only fix them.

Lesson 14
Spelling
1. Play hangman. Have someone play with you.
   - They will find the word to use for Lesson 14 in the answer key.
   - They will tell you how many letters are in the word. Draw that number of blanks on a piece of paper.
   - Guess one letter at a time. If the letter is in the word, have them tell you which blank or blanks it goes in. Write it in.
   - If you want, for each wrong guess, draw a piece of a picture. Try to guess the word before you finish your picture.
2. This one should be done without looking back!

Lesson 15
Spelling
1. Take the spelling test. Have someone read the words to you from the answers for Lesson 15.
2. Any word you spell incorrectly today, rewrite five times, correctly of course.

Lesson 16
Spelling
1. Have someone read your spelling words from the Lesson 16 answer page in the back of the Lesson Guide. Write them as best as you can.
2. Check them and write correctly any that were misspelled.
3. Figure out why you wrote what you did and how you can remember the correct way, maybe by pronouncing the word a little differently.
4. Then try writing those corrected words again without looking.

Lesson 17
Spelling
1. Work on your spelling.
2. This unscramble uses the words from Lesson 16, so you can peek back if necessary.
3. The point is to pay attention to how they are spelled.
4. When your work is checked, make sure the spelling of each word is checked.
5. Rewrite any that were spelled wrong; don't only fix them

Lesson 18
Spelling
1. Fill in the blanks.
2. Again, these are the same spelling words, so you can look back for a hint IF you can't figure out a word.
3. When your work is checked, make sure the spelling of each word is checked.
4. Rewrite any that were spelled wrong; don't only fix them.

Lesson 19
Spelling
1. Play hangman. Have someone play with you.
   - They will find the word to use for Lesson 19 in the answer key.
   - They will tell you how many letters are in the word. Draw that number of blanks on a piece of paper.
   - Guess one letter at a time. If the letter is in the word, have them tell you which blank or blanks it goes in. Write it in.
   - If you want, for each wrong guess, draw a piece of a picture. Try to guess the word before you finish your picture.
2. This one should be done without looking back!

Lesson 20

Spelling

1. Take the spelling test. Have someone read the words to you from the answer key for Lesson 20.
2. Any word you spell incorrectly today, rewrite five times, correctly of course.

Lesson 21

Spelling

1. Fill in the crossword puzzle.
2. You should probably use pencil. Count the number of letters and use the letters that appear in the puzzle and in two different words to help you figure it out.
3. You should always be paying attention to how words are spelled.

Lesson 22

Grammar

1. Play editor. Find the mistakes in the essay.
2. Check your answers. Make sure you understand if you got something wrong. If you don't understand, ask a parent. If no one knows why, ask online.

Lesson 23

Grammar

1. Play editor. Find the mistakes in the essay.
2. Check your answers. Make sure you understand if you got something wrong. If you don't understand, ask a parent. If no one knows why, ask online.

Lesson 24

Grammar

1. Play editor. Find the mistakes in the essay.
2. Check your answers. Make sure you understand if you got something wrong. If you don't understand, ask a parent. If no one knows why, ask online.

Lesson 25

Writing

1. Today you are writing. Write at least one paragraph.
2. Your paragraph must begin with an introductory, topic sentence. It must end with a conclusion.
3. Your topic is: If you could pick someone you know to be president, who would you pick and why?
4. That means your first sentence should be something along the lines of: If I could pick anyone I knew to be president, it would be…
   - When you are asked to answer a question, restate it so that the reader knows what question is being answered.
   - It's good form.

Lesson 26

Writing

1. You are going to write a dialog today.
2. Here are some dialog reminders. The punctuation always comes before the quotation marks. Each new speaker must begin on a new line.
   - "I can't," he said. (comma inside the quote and lowercase he)
   - He said, "You can." (comma before the quote and uppercase You)
   - "I won't!" he yelled. (lowercase he)
   - "You will!" He pointed firmly across the room. (uppercase He, no speech tag "said")
3. There is a prompt on the page for your dialog. While part of the point is to practice proper dialog form, the other point is to push you creatively. You can practice creativity just like you practice anything else to get better at it.

Lesson 27

Grammar

1. Play editor. Find the mistakes in the essay.
2. Check your answers. Make sure you understand if you got something wrong. If you don't understand, ask a parent. If no one knows why, ask online.

Lesson 28

Writing

1. Write an advertisement for the paper for the classifieds section.
2. You've lost a pet, or you are looking to buy an old _____ if someone has one to offer. What would you say? What would you ask for? What would you be willing to pay?

Lesson 29

Grammar

1. Play editor. Find the mistakes in the essay.
2. Check your answers. Make sure you understand if you got something wrong. If you don't understand, ask a parent. If no one knows why, ask online.
3. Play grammar gorilla.

Lesson 30

Grammar

1. Play editor. Find the mistakes in the essay.
2. Check your answers. Make sure you understand if you got something wrong. If you don't understand, ask a parent. If no one knows why, ask online.

Lesson 31

Writing

1. You will be doing a short writing today. Make sure you start with an introductory topic sentence.
2. You've just been elected president of the world. What will you do first? Why? How will you go about it?

Lesson 32
Grammar
1. Play editor. Find the mistakes in the essay.
2. Check your answers. Make sure you understand if you got something wrong. If you don't understand, ask a parent. If no one knows why, ask online.

Lesson 33
Grammar
1. Play editor. Find the mistakes in the essay.
2. Check your answers. Make sure you understand if you got something wrong. If you don't understand, ask a parent. If no one knows why, ask online.

Lesson 34
Writing
1. Write "a model letter to a friend on some subject of general interest."
2. Here's a how-to reminder on the form of a friendly letter.
    - You can see a little picture of a letter on the next page.
    - You need to include:
        - date
        - salutation (greeting)
        - body (the stuff you wanted to say)
        - closing (yours sincerely, love)
        - signature (name)

September, 1860

Dear Pa,

I know it will be a long time before you get this letter, but I wanted to write and tell you how much I miss you. Ma, Patricia, and I are doing well, but we miss you like crazy. We know you had to go back and help the others venture west, but we can't wait for you to be with us again. We pray daily for your safety.

You should have seen the size of the rabbit I snagged for dinner last night! It was the biggest one I've ever seen. We were able to share some meat with a few others, and Ma says the skins will make a nice, warm blanket for Patricia to use come winter. I'm doing my best to take care of them. I know you would be proud.

I'd better get this letter sealed and ready for transport. Daniel is traveling to meet the Pony Express rider in the morning, and I want to make sure this letter gets to you before you leave to come back to us.

Much love,

Jimmy

Lesson 35
Grammar
1. Play editor. Find the mistakes in the essay.
2. Check your answers. Make sure you understand if you got something wrong. If you don't understand, ask a parent. If no one knows why, ask online.
3. Answer the grammar questions.
    - The subject is what the sentence is about.
    - The simple subject is just the noun. The complete subject includes all the adjectives that described the noun.
    - The predicate is everything else in the sentence.
    - The simple predicate is just the verb.
    - An interrogative sentence is one asking a question.

Lesson 36
Writing
1. Today you are going to plan out a five-paragraph essay on a subject you are learning about or have just learned about for school.
2. Write in your topic. Don't choose something huge like ancient Egypt. Choose something specific like how the pyramids were made.
3. Start with the "main idea" boxes. What are three main points you can make about your topic?
    - Write in those three smaller topics.
4. Today you are going to list facts in the "supporting facts" boxes. Fill in as many as you can with at least two facts filled in for each column. The facts should be listed under the appropriate main idea.
5. Do a little more research if you have to.

Lesson 37
Writing
1. Today write the introduction for your essay. Typing it will make it easier to edit later. There is no worksheet page for this unless you want to use the space on the Lesson 36 page.
2. Your first sentence should get your reader's attention. Start with a question, an interesting quote, or a strange or amazing fact. Tell more about your topic but don't give away your facts yet. Then finish the paragraph with your **thesis statement**, the sentence that tells what your essay is about. Make sure your thesis is what your "main ideas" from Lesson 36 will tell about.
3. Your first paragraph needs to be 3-5 sentences long. My example below…

You've seen pictures of pyramids, right? Did you know that each stone in a pyramid weighed as much as a car? The pyramids were built with a lot of hard work, but also with a lot of intelligence. **The pyramids were an amazing feat of engineering.**

Lesson 38
Writing
1. Today write the first two of your paragraphs for the body of your essay. There is no separate worksheet for today. If you can, type this essay. It makes the most sense for editing.
2. Make sure you order your middle paragraphs so they flow with the most sense. Also make sure you use different types of sentences of different lengths.
3. The first sentence of each paragraph will be the topic sentence for that paragraph; it will tell what that paragraph is about. Then you will state the facts and any commentary you have. The last sentence is not only the concluding sentence for the paragraph but also the transition to the next paragraph. Below is an example. What was the transition sentence I used to get from workers to the inclined plane? How does it make the transition?

> (topic sentence) You might imagine that the pyramids were made by slaves, but really they were built by paid workers. (Then some facts…) Not only did the workers get paid enough to lead comfortable lives, but new technology made their work easier as well.

> (topic sentence for the next paragraph) The inclined plane was, at the time, an ingenious way to get the incredibly heavy stones up the pyramid.

> Answers: ("Not only did the workers get paid enough to lead comfortable lives, but new technology made their work easier as well." The sentence mentions content from the current paragraph and the following paragraph.)

Lesson 39
Writing
1. Write the third paragraph for the body of your essay. Make sure it transitions with the one before it. Use the instructions from Lesson 38.
2. Write the conclusion to your essay. The *first* sentence of your conclusion should restate your **thesis**. Do NOT use the same wording.
3. Sum up what you have shared in your essay. Give some commentary on the subject. This needs to be 1 to 3 sentences.
4. The last sentence of the paragraph should tell us why you wrote about it, what's so important about this, why should we care about this…Make some sort of statement. Here's my example.

> I think the pyramids prove that God was right when he decided to confuse the languages of the people on earth. "Nothing they plan to do will be impossible for them." (Genesis 11:6b NIV1984)

Lesson 40
Writing
1. Edit your essay.
2. In your workbook is an editing checklist.
3. You could consider finding a peer to read your essay to give you feedback. You could give them the editing checklist as well.
4. Print your essay when you are sure it's your best. Ask a parent to add it to your portfolio.

Lesson 41
Writing
1. Design a t-shirt for yourself, one that you would wear every day for a week so that everyone would see what it says and what's on it.
2. What would it look like? What would it say? What would wearing it say about you?

Lesson 42
Writing
1. You are going to be writing a book review. Choose a book you've recently read.
2. Read the example of a book review that follows.
   - Think of these things as you write.
     - Did the book have a point?
     - Was the writing descriptive, exciting, etc.?
     - What are the good and bad points of the books?
     - What did you think of the book?
     - Would you recommend it? Why or why not?
   - You'll want to include these things.
     - an interesting introduction
     - thesis that includes your recommendation about the book
     - brief summary in present tense
     - body paragraphs all start with a topic sentence and end with a transition
     - include examples from the book, try to add a quote if you can
     - conclusion with your thoughts
3. Today you are going to write your introduction. Remember to start with something interesting, not to give away your facts yet, and to end with your thesis.

Book Review Example

Would you enjoy reading a book that is an exciting work of high fantasy and also a description of amazing things that can happen in our everyday real lives? *The Voyage of the Dawn Treader* by C. S. Lewis is an excellent book because it is not only a riveting adventure but also gives a beautiful picture of faith and redemption.

Edmund and Lucy Pevensie, along with their unpleasant cousin Eustace, are transported through a painting of a ship from England to another world called Narnia, which Edmund and Lucy had visited before. They land in the sea and are taken up onto a Narnian ship, where Edmund and Lucy find their old friend Caspian, who is now King of Narnia. The three children accompany the ship and its crew on their quest through the unknown eastern seas. Caspian is seeking the seven Narnian lords who were exiled years before by his evil uncle, and he is also seeking to find the eastern edge of the world. The group undergoes many adventures and hardships on the islands they encounter on their quest. They do eventually either find the missing lords, or discover how they died and also find the end of the world.

This book is an enthralling adventure and especially appeals to those who love exploration. The crew of the Dawn Treader, along with Edmund, Lucy, and Eustace, encounter new environments on each island they land on as they journey farther and farther from Narnia, and also face unique challenges on each one. On the first island they tangle with slave traders. On the second they discover dragon's treasure and Eustace, through greed, turns into a dragon. On other islands they find a pool that turns whatever touches it to gold, or encounter invisible enemies, and a magician's castle, and an island where nightmares come true.

One of the best things about this book is that it is not only an exciting and fast-moving adventure; there are also themes of faith and redemption throughout it. There is a character named Aslan who appears in the form of a lion and reminds me of Jesus. Some of the other characters have faith in him, and sometimes he appears to help them or correct them. Once he appeared to Eustace, who had been turned into a dragon, and tears away his dragon skin, turning him into a boy again and giving him new clothes. This scene is such a clear and moving picture of how a person can be rescued and transformed by Jesus.

The Voyage of the Dawn Treader is one of my favorite books because it is not only an exciting adventure, but also has inspiring pictures of faith and redemption throughout. The way that Aslan encounters and transforms the characters inspires the reader to think more deeply about Jesus and about himself or herself. I love the way Edmund describes Aslan: "He is the great Lion, the son of the Emperor-over-Sea, who saved me and saved Narnia. We've all seen him. Lucy sees him most often. And it may be Aslan's country we're sailing to" (475). This book is one that I never grow tired of and has had a big effect on my life.

Lesson 43
Grammar
1. There is a worksheet for today, before you get to your writing.
2. If you don't want to write out each word, create abbreviations for the words.
3. You'll be identifying the words by their parts of speech. Choose the part of speech that the word would most commonly be used as.
    - noun, adverb, adjective, pronoun, verb, preposition
    - Running is typically an action verb. It could be a noun: running is good exercise.

Writing
1. Today you are going to write the book summary and the following paragraph.
2. Make sure you are following the example and using all instructions for your writing. Your writing should be about the same length as the example. Make sure you use a variety of sentence types and lengths.

Lesson 44
Writing
1. Today you will write another paragraph and your conclusion.
2. Make sure you are following the example and using all instructions for your writing. Your writing should be about the same length as the example. Make sure you use a variety of sentence types and lengths.

Grammar
1. You are going to be identifying parts of speech by their usage in the sentence.
2. Basketball is a noun, but basketball in the phrase basketball game is being used as an adjective, telling us what kind of game it is.

Lesson 45

Writing

1. Reread the example. Read your book review and use the instructions in Lesson 42 as a checklist to see if your review has those things. If you are missing something, edit your review and add it.
2. Read your review out loud. Edit anything that sounds awkward.
3. Check your spelling, punctuation, etc. Make sure the title of the book is underlined or written in *italics*.

Lesson 46

Spelling/Grammar

1. Today is mostly about the letter S. You are going to practice possessives and plurals.
2. Possessives are shown with an apostrophe and show that something belongs to someone.
   - The kid's bike.
   - The kids' bike.
     - The first one shows that the kid, the one kid has a bike.
     - The second one shows that the kids, the many kids have a bike that they share.
   - The person's choice is clear.
   - The people's choice is clear.
     - They both get an S added on, even though the one is already plural. The S in the case of possessives show possession, not plurality.
   - However, in the case of pronouns, the possessives do NOT have an apostrophe.
     - It's means it is.
     - Its is the possessive saying something belongs to it.
3. Complete your worksheet. At the bottom are plurals. See if you remember the spelling rules.
   - If you get any wrong, practice them the correct way and look up other words that use the same spelling pattern.

Lesson 47

Grammar

1. Play editor. Find the mistakes in the essay.
2. Check your answers. Make sure you understand if you got something wrong. If you don't understand, ask a parent. If no one knows why, ask online.

Lesson 48

Writing

1. Write a summary of the story of Little Red Riding Hood. Can you do it in one great sentence?

Grammar

1. Play editor. Find the mistakes in the essay.
2. Check your answers. Make sure you understand if you got something wrong. If you don't understand, ask a parent. If no one knows why, ask online.

Lesson 49

Grammar

1. Play editor. Find the mistakes in the essay.
2. Check your answers. Make sure you understand if you got something wrong. If you don't understand, ask a parent. If no one knows why, ask online.

Lesson 50

Writing

1. Write what happens next in a favorite book of yours. What happens after the story ends?
2. Continue the story. This is a creative writing assignment. Have fun with it.

Lesson 51

Spelling

1. Fill in the puzzle.
2. Use the letters there and the lengths of the words to help you.

Lesson 52

Grammar

1. You are going to label the parts of speech.
   - Though some call A AN THE adjectives, here they will be labeled articles.
   - Label names as proper nouns, not just nouns.
2. Then check your answers.
3. The second part of your worksheet is about subjects and predicates.
   - The simple subject is the noun, who/what the sentence is about. The complete subject is everything that goes with the noun, such as adjectives.
   - The simple predicate is the verb that goes with the subject, telling us what the subject is or does. The complete predicate is everything that's not part of the subject.
   - Every word in a sentence is either part of the subject or the predicate.

Lesson 53
Spelling
1. Complete the word search.
2. Pay attention to how the words are spelled. If there are words you don't know how to pronounce, find out how.

Lesson 54
Grammar
1. You'll be doing some more with subjects and predicates.
2. Remember that prepositions always come in phrases. Prepositions have to do with location. They are always followed by nouns or pronouns.
3. Look at this sentence: Reading *The Call of the Wild* is one of my favorite parts of the day.
   - Reading looks like a verb, but it is the subject, in fact, reading is a noun in this sentence. It's a special kind of noun called a **gerund**.
   - **Gerunds** are *ing* words that function as nouns.
4. Here's another example: Finding the treasure would be amazing!
5. Finding the treasure is the subject and finding is the **gerund**, a noun.
6. Complete your worksheet.

Lesson 55
Writing
1. Write for at least fifteen minutes. Go!
   - Write the end of a chapter or
   - write a short story or
   - write as the "I" character in your story or...

Lesson 56
Spelling/Writing
1. Play hangman. Have someone play with you.
   - They will find the word to use for Lesson 56 in the answer key.
   - They will tell you how many letters are in the word. Draw that number of blanks on a piece of paper.
   - Guess one letter at a time. If the letter is in the word, have them tell you which blank or blanks it goes in. Write it in.
   - If you want, for each wrong guess, draw a piece of a picture. Try to guess the word before you finish your picture.
2. The answers are phrases, expressions.

Lesson 57
Spelling
1. Complete the word search.
2. Remember to think about the words and learn how to pronounce them if you don't know them already.

Lesson 58
Grammar
1. Which of these contains a **gerund**? How is the ING word used in each sentence? Reminder: **Gerunds** are *ing* words that function as nouns.
    *   Smashing against rocks and snags, they veered into the bank.
    *   Whining was his only response.
    *   Writhing muscles strained at the load.
        Answers: verb, noun/gerund, adjective

Lesson 59
Grammar
1. Write five gerund sentences.
2. Use the ING word as a noun, as the subject.

Lesson 60
Writing
1. Write for at least fifteen minutes.
2. Go! Just write!

Lesson 61
Writing
1. Rewrite the ending of a book you've recently read. What would have made a better ending?
2. This is a creative writing excitement. Have fun.

Lesson 62
Writing
1. This week you'll be writing a personal response to a book you have recently finished for school. If you haven't recently finished one, you'll have to choose a novel you've read to write about. You will be following the example.
2. Read the example on the following page. You may have seen this before.
3. Today decide on your thesis, two key points, and look for textual evidence.

The Voyage of the Dawn Treader

The Voyage of the Dawn Treader, by C.S. Lewis, is one of the most moving and exciting books I have ever read. Edmund and Lucy Pevensie, along with their unpleasant cousin Eustace, are transported through a painting of a ship from England to another world called Narnia, which Edmund and Lucy had visited before. They land in the sea and are taken up onto a Narnian ship, where Edmund and Lucy find their old friend Caspian, who is now King of Narnia. The three children accompany the ship and its crew on their quest through the unknown eastern seas. Caspian is seeking the seven Narnian lords who were exiled years before by his evil uncle, and also seeking to find the eastern edge of the world. The group undergoes many adventures and hardships on the islands they encounter on their quest. They do eventually find all of the missing lords, or discover how they died, and also find the end of the world. While the novel is an exciting story, it is also more than that. The ideas of faith and redemption are all through the story, making me feel that in a way the events of the story are tied in to real life.

The book is a story of faith in Aslan. Edmund and Lucy always have faith in Aslan, a great talking lion who represents Jesus Christ in the Narnia stories. For example, Lucy is afraid to go into the mysterious magician's mansion on one of the islands, but she has to in order to find and say the spell that will make the Dufflepuds, the invisible inhabitants of the island, visible again. She trusts Aslan to take care of her and help her and even sees Aslan and talks with him in the mansion when she needs him most.

At the end of the story, the children and a few of the others meet Aslan in person at the end of the world, which turns out to be the entrance to Aslan's country, like heaven. He sends Lucy and Edmund back to their own world, telling them they will never come back to Narnia. When they are upset and protest about never seeing him again, he tells them that they will get to know him by another name in their own world.

The book is also full of the idea of redemption, or being saved from something bad and or changed into something good. The most moving example was on one of the islands the ship landed on, where Eustace, who had been a complaining, stealing bully so far on the journey, finds a dragon's treasure, and gets magically turned into a dragon himself because of his greed. He lets the others know what happened, and is able to help them because of his new size and strength. Later Aslan comes and meets him and tears away his dragon skin and turns him into a boy again.

In the magician's mansion, Aslan saved Lucy from giving in to the temptation to say a spell which would make her beautiful. We learn that Lucy has been jealous of her sister Susan's beauty and almost says a spell which would have made her beautiful but also would have caused a lot of destruction. At that moment Aslan shows up and corrects and comforts Lucy, saving her from making a mistake which would have ended up causing a lot of pain.

The idea of faith and redemption run through the whole book. And although the book is full of magical events, talking animals, and exciting adventures, for me it still is very personal and real because these ideas are real in my life and my world. After all, the real main character of the book is Aslan, and he is in our world as well as in Narnia. He's just known by another name here.

Lesson 63
Writing
1. Write your introduction and first point section. Use the example as a guideline.
2. There are no worksheets for these days while you are writing the personal response.

Lesson 64
Writing
1. Write your second point.
2. Then write your conclusion.

Lesson 65

Writing

1. Edit your report. There's an editing checklist in your workbook.
2. Read it out loud. Make sure it is spelled correctly and punctuated correctly. Make sure you use a variety of sentence structures. Use long and short sentences. Change some words to make better choices.
3. When you are pleased with your work, print it out and share it.
4. This might be something you want to add to your portfolio.

Lesson 66

Spelling

1. Complete the spelling crossword. All of the words follow the spelling rule: I before E except after C.
2. You might want to add it to your portfolio to show spelling.

Lesson 67

Grammar

1. This is a simple worksheet to practice punctuation.
2. An interrogative sentence asks a question. An imperative sentence is a command.

Lesson 68

Grammar

1. Another type of sentence can start with an -ing verb, but in this case, it is used as an adjective. It is called a **participle**. Your job is to make sure your participles don't dangle. Here's what I mean.
2. *Tying his shoe, the boy was very proud of his accomplishment.*
3. *Tying his shoe* is the **participle**; technically, *tying* is the participle and *tying his shoe* is the **participle phrase**.
4. The **participle** is describing *the boy*. The **participle phrase** is always followed by a comma and then the thing it is describing.
   - If the next word/words don't tell you what the participle is describing, then we call that a dangling participle. It's just hanging out there all by itself. That's a no-no. Don't do it.
   - The word after the comma must be the noun being described.
5. Here are some more examples:
   - Getting home on time, she raced inside to make sure she didn't miss anything.
   - Finishing the last lap, he raised his arms in victory.
   - Panting, the dog circled his bed and flopped down.
      - What are the participle phrases in the examples above and what do they modify (describe)? (Answers)

Answers: Getting home on time describes she. Finishing the last lap describes he. Panting describes the dog.

Lesson 69

Grammar

1. Write three sentences with **participle phrases**.
2. Here are Lesson 68 's examples:

- Getting home on time, she raced inside to make sure she didn't miss anything.
- Finishing the last lap, he raised his arms in victory.
- Panting, the dog circled his bed and flopped down.
3. Now I'm going to rewrite the participles as **gerunds.**
   - Getting home on time was important to her.
   - Finishing the last lap was the mark of victory.
   - Panting was the dog's way of showing he was tired.
4. On your worksheet, you'll be writing particle phrases and gerunds.

Lesson 70
Writing
1. Write a short story in your workbook using at least one gerund and one participle.
2. If you use more of any of those, get a high five and/or hug.

Lesson 71
Grammar
1. Can you answer these questions about nouns?
2. It's okay if you don't know it all. You can learn from what you get wrong!

Lesson 72
Writing
1. You are going to begin writing a descriptive piece. Read the following example.
2. Choose what you are going to describe.
3. Your goal should be for your descriptive essay to be as long as this example, but you aren't going to start writing just yet. There is no worksheet for today.

Peeling A Mandarin

Peeling a mandarin involves all five senses. To pick up a mandarin is to shiver with anticipation and to hesitate before taking the plunge into strange, intense, striking, wildly different types of touch, smell, taste, sound, and sight. The act of peeling and eating a mandarin is a rollercoaster ride of sensations.

First, I slowly pull the skin off a sweet, small, juicy mandarin. The peel pushes back against the pull of my hand. Its push is broken when the skin tears. The tear of the skin makes a soft, faint, steady, satisfying sound. I put it closer to my head and tear the peel slowly again and again. My face is hit with its intensely sweet acidic sting. My fingers squeeze down on the soft white foam inside the peel. They dig into the waxy, smooth, pungent, bumpy orange exterior.

The entire mandarin is peeled, a soft, delicate, slightly heavy ball, dull orange with soft white padding. I peel off some strips of white for a purer color. I carefully, gingerly grasp the soft ball like a water balloon, a thin waterproof skin holding in an explosion of juice. I hold it up to a window. It is infused with bluish skylight, slightly dulling the orange. I hold it up to a lamp with golden light, a lamp with a dark orange-brown lampshade. The mandarin is radiant with glowing light. It glows a vivid ball of orange, intense like a sunrise. My face is once again hit with its intensely sweet acidic sting as I slowly break it into segments. I pick up a segment and hold it up to the light. It is yellower than the whole ball together. I can see the individual veins and a seed, standing out dark against the glowing yellow. I put the segment into my mouth and bite through the delicate balloon-skin. It explodes into an intense, stunning, acidic stream of juice.

I put my fingers up to my face and breathe in the pungent odor of the waxy oily mandarin skin. I rub my fingers together and feel the strange feeling of the juice that is on them. Taking your time to experience something completely is good for you. When you take your time, you will be amazed at the things you discover around you.

Lesson 73
Writing
1. Today write two similes and two metaphors that describe aspects of your topic.
2. Remember: similes and metaphors compare two unlike things. Metaphors call one thing the other. Similes use *like* or *as*.
3. Here are some examples from the essay.
   - like a water balloon
   - like a sunrise

Lesson 74
Writing
1. Reread the example.
2. Write a paragraph of VIVID description.
3. Write a list of specific verbs and great adjectives that can be used to describe your topic. Then list words that describe the smell, taste, sound, and feel of your topic.

Lesson 75
Writing
1. Reread the first paragraph of the example.
2. Now write your first paragraph. Make sure you have a clearly stated topic sentence.
3. This should be typed if possible because we'll be working on this over several days.

Lesson 76
Spelling
1. Do the word search in your workbook.
Writing
1. Write another paragraph. Remember to use similes, metaphors, and vivid descriptions.
2. Look at the list of what you wrote in Lesson 73.

Lesson 77
Grammar
1. Play editor. Find the mistakes in the essay.
2. Check your answers. Make sure you understand if you got something wrong. If you don't understand, ask a parent. If no one knows why, ask online.

Writing
1. Write another paragraph. Your description should end up longer than the example.
2. Remember to use similes, metaphors and vivid descriptions. Look at the list of what you wrote in Lesson 73.

Lesson 78

Grammar
  1. Play editor. Find the mistakes in the essay.
  2. Check your answers. Make sure you understand if you got something wrong. If you don't understand, ask a parent. If no one knows why, ask online.

Writing
  1. Read the second two paragraphs of the essay.
  2. Write another paragraph. Remember to use similes, metaphors, and vivid descriptions.

Lesson 79

Grammar
  1. Play editor. Find the mistakes in the essay.
  2. Check your answers. Make sure you understand if you got something wrong. If you don't understand, ask a parent. If no one knows why, ask online.

Writing
  1. Write another paragraph.
  2. Remember to use similes, metaphors and vivid descriptions.

Lesson 80

Writing
  1. Read the last paragraph of the example of descriptive writing.
  2. Write your conclusion.
  3. How long is your essay?
  4. Print out your draft. That means print out your descriptive writing you've been working on. A draft means that it's not in its final form.

Lesson 81

Writing
  1. Read this lesson on word choice.

Word choice is about choosing the perfect words. Here are some things to think about when choosing your words.
Use just the words you need. No need to use a lot of filler words. Just say what you mean. "I think…" instead of "I am of the opinion that perhaps…"

Use specific words.
  • Adjectives
    • decaying instead of old
    • honest and dependable instead of good
    • like blushing cheeks instead of red
  • Verbs
    • sprinted instead of ran
    • grumbled instead of said
    • flopped instead of sat
  • Nouns
    • poodle instead of dog

- cottage instead of house
- lemonade instead of drink

Use all the senses. Describe how things looked, felt, smelled, tasted, and sounded.
Use metaphors and similes.
Use sentences with action verbs.

- The yard was covered with snow becomes the snow covered the yard. Or, the snow covered the yard like a blanket.

Practice
- What would be a better word to replace each of these?
  - bad (adjective)
  - smelled (verb)
  - coat (noun)

2. Read through your descriptive paper and make changes in your word choice.

Grammar
1. Look at this sentence. I left a blank intentionally.
   - Eating certain foods _____ make us "unclean", unholy.
2. What is the subject? (Answers)
3. What should the verb be: don't or doesn't? (Answers)
4. What kind of noun is the subject of this sentence? (Answers)

Lesson 82
Writing
1. Read this lesson on sentence.

When you combine sentences into stories and reports, they should flow together naturally. Here are some things to think about when writing.
Sentences should be of different lengths.

- Some should be short.
- Some should be longer, and they should include more information since there's always more to tell.

Related, the sentences should be of different types.

- Some should tell.
- Some should ask, why?
- Some should exclaim!

Sentences should start in different ways.

- Then I…should never be used, and certainly not in every sentence!
- Sentence starters can include: after coming home, while we were there, forgetting what time it was, if you think,…

Sentences should connect with transitions.

- Try using connecting words such as however, although, unfortunately, etc.

Practice
- Think of a sentence that starts with while.

- Change this sentence into an interrogative (a question). We will miss them when they are gone.

2. Read through your descriptive paper. Underline all of your first words. Circle all of your connector words.
3. Do you have any interrogative, imperative, or exclamatory sentences? If not, you should try to add at least one of each. You don't have to add new sentences. You can change what you have.
4. Do you have any really short sentences? Do you have any really long sentences? You should have both. Add them. Make changes.
5. Make sure your sentence length varies throughout your paper. Do you use while, as, when, since…?

Lesson 83
Writing
1. Read about conventions.

Conventions are the mechanics of writing, the capital letters, the punctuation. They are correct grammar and spelling. They are knowing when to start a new paragraph because you are introducing a new idea.

Make sure you capitalize the first letter in each sentence and nothing else except proper nouns (the names of people, places, and things).

Make sure each sentence ends with a punctuation mark and that you don't just run multiple sentences together without a break.

Add a comma after an introductory part of a sentence, and add one before a conjunction, like I just did. I also just added a comma to separate off unnecessary information.

Make sure to keep using the same verb tense. Don't start using present tense and then change to using past.

Here are some proofreading marks that you can use on your papers when you edit them.

¶ new paragraph

^ insert something

2. Use the strategies listed to read through your paper and look for corrections.

Lesson 84
Writing
1. Read through these writing techniques that you should keep in mind.

These are the areas you need to think about when writing.

1. Content
   - have a clear topic
   - start with a topic sentence that states your main idea
   - use only details that support your main idea
2. Organization
   - ideas flow together
   - transitions connect sentences
   - introduction and conclusion
3. Voice
   - tone engages the reader
   - words are comfy and inviting or exciting and draw you in
4. Word Choice
   - great specific words that let the reader see what you are seeing
5. Varied Sentences
   - sentences of different lengths and types
6. Conventions
   - proper use of grammar and spelling

2. What changes can you make so that your paper would get a perfect score?
3. Add your name, date, and title to the top of your paper.

Lesson 85
Writing
1. Read through the rubric in your workbook.
2. Would your paper get a perfect score? If not, make changes.
3. When you are entirely pleased, print it out.
4. Give it to a parent to add to your portfolio.

Lesson 86
Spelling
1. Do you remember your spelling words? Have someone read you the list from the answer key section, while you fill in the blanks.
2. Fix and then rewrite correctly any that you misspell.
Writing
1. This week you are going to start working on an essay comparing and contrasting two things.
2. When you compare two things, you talk about how they are similar. You may use words such as like, similar, the same as, both, in common, as well as.
3. When you contrast two things, you talk about how they are different. You may use words such as unlike, as opposed to, however, although, on the other hand, while, instead.
4. Transition words will help you lead from one point to another.
   - While spring and fall may have similar temperatures, each has a unique feel. In spring we are waiting impatiently for warmer weather to come, whereas in the fall we embrace the cooler weather and welcome the chance to drink cocoa and hot cider.

Lesson 87

Grammar

1. There's a parts-of-speech worksheet for you today.

Writing

1. Your new writing assignment will be to compare and contrast two things.
2. Read the example that follows.
3. Choose your topic. I suggest using something from your science or history studies so that you already have the information you need.
   - You could compare and contrast the Romans and Greeks, two inventors, two elements, two countries, two presidents…
4. Fill in the compare and contrast sheet in your workbook with as many ideas as you can come up with. You don't have to use them all in your essay. Just brainstorm and write as many things as you can.

There are two countries that I lived in for more than a handful of years, apart from America, the country of my birth. Some things about these places, one in Europe and one in Asia, are similar, and others are very different. Macedonia and Turkey are two countries that I've enjoyed calling home, even though only one really feels like home.

Macedonia is a Balkan country nestled above Greece in southern Europe. Like Turkey, it was an area that was ruled by the Ottomans. Both have ruins of fortresses built by the Ottomans during their reign. Turkish coffee is the most common drink in Macedonia. It's not, however, commonly drunk in Turkey. Tea is the drink of choice there like in other Middle Eastern countries.

Also, like other Middle Eastern countries, Turkey is an Islamic country. Macedonia, on the other hand, is an Orthodox Christian country. However, Macedonia is about a third Muslim, as a third of the country is of another ethnic group. Turkey, on the other hand is much more homogenous, as nearly all living there would call themselves Muslim.

This difference is even more deeply felt as Macedonia is a very small country, while Turkey is a relatively large one. The population of Turkey is approaching eighty million, while Macedonia's is just two million. A quarter of the population of Macedonia lives in the capital city leaving large parts of the country undeveloped, perfect for exploration, hikes, and picnics, some of our family's favorite things.

Both countries are similar in their laid-back lifestyle where people spend hours together over a hot drink, but in Turkey it's mostly the men who get to do this. They both value time spent with friends and family. Neither country is wealthy and meals often are built around staples such as tomatoes and peppers. One difference in cuisine is the base of rice in Turkey and that of potatoes in Macedonia. Turkey offers much more spicy food as well, also a nod to their Middle East ties.

There are things I enjoy about each country. I'm a tea drinker, but I can't eat spicy food. I enjoy the slower pace of life in these countries and the time spent visiting as a family. Our family fits into Muslim culture with our modest dress and lots of children, but an Islamic atmosphere can be oppressive. In Macedonia we got to come in and out of that atmosphere as we pleased, whereas in Turkey there was no escape from it. It's Macedonia with its smaller size, fewer people, more open space, that has my heart as a place I'd call home.

Lesson 88

Writing

1. Today you need to figure out the three main points you are going to make. These will be your three middle paragraphs.
2. For these three things you will show how they are the same and where they differ. If you were doing two countries, you could say, "Even though they are both in South America, they have very different climates." "While both countries use Spanish as an official language, their native languages are very different." "Some foods are eaten in both regions, but other dishes are unique to each locale." These are just some ideas off the top of my head to show you. I didn't have any specific countries in mind. I was just making it up.
3. Use your sheet from Lesson 87 and pair up three similarities and differences and write out three sentences like I just did.

Lesson 89

Grammar

1. You are going to be identifying the type of noun between concrete and abstract.
2. Basically, a concrete noun you can touch.
3. Abstract nouns are things like ideas, actions, and qualities.

Writing

1. Today you will write your introduction.
2. Your introduction should start with an interesting quote, question, or comment. Then provide background information on your two topics. Finally, conclude with your thesis statement. Your thesis statement will include the three things you are going to compare/contrast, your three points. List these three points in the order you are going to talk about them in your essay.
3. Use the sample in Lesson 87 as a guide.

Lesson 90

Grammar

1. Here are the plural spelling rules. Use them to refresh your memory and then complete your worksheet page for today.
    *   -fe becomes -ves as in life to lives
    *   -f becomes -ves as in half to halves (but not always: stuff/stuffs)
    *   -o becomes -oes as in tomato to tomatoes (but not always: piano/pianos)
    *   -us becomes -i as in nucleus to nuclei (but not always: octopus/octopuses)
    *   -is becomes -es as in crisis to crises
    *   -on becomes -a as in phenomenon to phenomena (but not always: son/sons)
    *   Some change vowels man/men. Some just change person/people. Some stay the same sheep.
    *   These are general rules and I have shown just some exceptions to the rules.

Writing

1. Write your second paragraph. It should be on the point you list first in your thesis statement.

2. Make sure to include examples. You can't just say what is different; you have to show what is different.

Lesson 91
Writing
1. Write your third paragraph. It should be on the second point you list in your thesis statement. If you need inspiration, check out the example essay again in Lesson 87.
2. Make sure your first sentence is your topic sentence for the paragraph.
3. Make sure to include examples. You can't just say what is different; you have to show what is different.

Lesson 92
Grammar
1. Play editor. Find the mistakes in the essay.
2. Check your answers. Make sure you understand if you got something wrong. If you don't understand, ask a parent. If no one knows why, ask online.
Writing
1. Write the last paragraph for the body of your essay. It should be on the last point you list in your thesis statement.
2. Make sure to include examples. You can't just say what is different; you have to show what is different.

Lesson 93
Grammar
1. Rewrite the incorrect paragraphs.
2. Look for spelling mistakes and a couple punctuation mistakes. What's supposed to be capitalized?
Writing
1. Write your conclusion. What elements does a conclusion have?
2. Make sure you end with a good closing statement that wraps up the essay. Don't just let it end. You know how in a lot of movies they make sure you know what happens to each character? They know people like things tied up neatly in a pretty bow. Don't leave loose ends. Tie up your essay in a pretty bow. Write a closing statement that will leave us with a good feeling inside, just like those movies.

Lesson 94
Grammar
1. Complete this pronoun exercise in your workbook. Do you know what the subject of a sentence is? Subject pronouns are I, you, he, she, it, we, and they.
2. Check your answers and understand what the correct answer should be before you are done for the day.
Writing
1. Use the editing checklist in your workbook to edit your essay.
2. Read your essay out loud and change anything that doesn't sound right.

3. Make changes! Make sure you have long and short sentences that start in different ways. Do any of your sentences start with participles? They should. Do you use the words "like," "since," and "however?" You should.

Lesson 95
Grammar
1. Complete the pronoun exercise in your workbook.
2. Objects come after prepositions and verbs. Object pronouns include: me, you, him, her, it, us, and them.

Writing
1. Use the scoring rubric in your workbook to edit your essay.
2. Edit your essay until it would get a perfect score.
3. When you are ready, print out your essay. Save it for your portfolio.

Lesson 96
English
1. Answer the writing review questions in the workbook.
2. Some reminders:
   - an independent clause can stand alone as a sentence, while a dependent one cannot
   - two independent clauses combined with a conjunction is a compound sentence, while an independent and dependent clause combine to form a complex sentence

Lesson 97
Grammar
1. Complete the pronoun exercise. Pay attention to the right answer if you get any wrong.
2. Remember the difference between subject and object pronouns. Also remember that an apostrophe with a pronoun means a contraction. It's means it is.
3. You can read the lesson below to do the bottom portion of your worksheet.

Writing
1. Read this lesson on the organization of your writing.
2. Complete the bottom section of your workbook page for today.

Organization is an important key to writing. It holds it all together. Here are some things to keep in mind.

- stories should have a beginning, middle, and end
- instructions should go in order from first to last
- an effect should come after a cause
- use your best reason last when trying to convince someone

Part of all this is deciding what you are trying to write. Are you writing a narrative story? Are you writing an argument to try to persuade someone to your opinion? Are you trying to teach someone how to do something? Are you trying to explain the outcome of an experiment or event?

When organizing your writing, know what type of writing you are doing, choose an organizational strategy, and then put it together with transition words such as first, lastly, and now.

Lesson 98
Grammar
1. Try this pronoun exercise. Check your answers. Change any errors to make them correct and stop to understand what makes it correct.

Writing
1. Read this lesson on voice.
2. Complete the bottom portion of the worksheet for today.

Your voice is your personality showing through your writing. It tells the reader how confident you are about your topic and how much you care. It can tell if you are being professional or laid back.

Part of voice is knowing your audience. Are you presenting research and need to sound like you know your stuff? Are you addressing peers who want to be entertained?

Your voice needs to match the occasion. If you are writing dialog, would the person say, "It's not gonna happen," as opposed to, "It is not going to happen," or "I should say with utmost certainty that it will not occur."

You can make your voice more interesting by adding descriptive language. "It was good" is not a strong voice. It will not engage your reader to keep reading. If you are bored writing, then your reader is probably bored reading. Challenge yourself and push yourself to engage with your writing so that your readers will be engaged as well.

Lesson 99
Grammar
1. Try the pronoun exercise in your workbook.
2. Remember to look to see if pronouns are being used as subjects or objects. When a pronoun is used along with a name, a trick is to take out the name and listen to which pronoun sounds correct.

Writing
1. You read about word choice in Lesson 81.
2. Complete the little word choice activity in your workbook to help you remember to pay attention to your word choice.

Lesson 100
Grammar
1. Try the different sort of pronoun exercise in your workbook.
2. A pronoun reference error is when the pronoun is referring to the wrong thing or you can't tell what the pronoun is referring to.

Writing
1. You read about sentences in Lesson 82 if you need to refer back. Complete the chart on your worksheet for today.
2. You can use your compare and contrast essay or descriptive piece.

Lesson 101
Writing
1. Choose a book you have recently finished reading or one you know well. You are going to be writing a book report on it.
2. You have today and Lesson 102. Today you'll write the introduction and the next two paragraphs.
3. Here's what you need to include.
   - Introduction should include the title and author, when the book was published, how long it is, what genre of book it is (comedy, fantasy, non-fiction, mystery…), the author's purpose or theme, and a main-idea sentence introducing your book report.
   - Describe the setting, characters, and mood of the story.
   - Summarize the story briefly.

Lesson 102
Writing
1. Finish writing your book report. You are going to write at least one paragraph explaining your analysis of the book. Then you'll finish with a conclusion.
   - Was the writing impactful?
   - What were the strengths and weaknesses of the book?
   - What did you think about the book? Was it exciting? Was it inspiring?
   - Would you recommend it? Explain why or why not.
   - Conclude with your thoughts on the book, what you are taking away from reading it and what you want your reader to know about it.
2. Read your book report out loud and make corrections.
3. Make sure it covers what is required.

Lesson 103
Spelling
1. Review the spelling rules and try the worksheet.
   - -fe becomes -ves as in life to lives
   - -f becomes -ves as in half to halves (but not always: stuff/stuffs)
   - -o becomes -oes as in tomato to tomatoes (but not always: piano/pianos)
   - -us becomes -i as in nucleus to nuclei (but not always: octopus/octopuses)
   - -is becomes -es as in crisis to crises
   - -on becomes -a as in phenomenon to phenomena (but not always: son/sons)
   - Some change vowels man/men. Some just change person/people. Some stay the same sheep.
   - These are general rules and I have shown just some exceptions to the rules.

Lesson 104
Grammar
1. Complete the worksheet for today on plurals and possessives.
   - plurals: dog –> dogs
   - possessives: dog's
   - plural possessive: dogs'
2. Pay attention to the clues in the sentence about whether or not the word is plural.

Lesson 105
Grammar
1. Complete your workbook page for today.
2. This is a continuing practice on plurals and possessives. You can look at Lesson 104's reminders.

Lesson 106
Spelling
1. Take a quiz.
2. Have someone read you the words from the answer key.

Lesson 107
Grammar
1. Complete the workbook page on apostrophes.
2. Apostrophes are used to make contractions, where two words are combined into one, and to show possession. They are NOT needed with possessive pronouns such as your book.
Writing
1. You're sailing the seven seas (as they say). Write a day's entry from the ship's log. There is no page for this. You'll be continuing this story over several days.
2. It doesn't have to be long, but make it exciting!

Lesson 108
Grammar
1. What's the difference between loose and lose?
   - Lose is a verb talking about something being lost.
   - Loose is an adjective describing something not being tight.
2. Complete the workbook page.
Writing
1. Write a day's log from the ship. Make it fascinating!
2. Continue with your story from Lesson 107.

Lesson 109
Grammar
1. Complete the who/whom activity on the workbook page for today.
2. Who is the subject. Whom is an object.
   - I should give it to whom? Next to whom will I be sitting?
Writing
1. You've landed on an island. Describe the setting of the island.
2. Continue your story.

Lesson 110

Writing

1. Turns out there are mutinous pirates on the island. What are you going to do? Continue your story.
2. There is no workbook page for today.

Lesson 111

Spelling

1. Find the spelling mistakes on the workbook page for today.
2. You are only looking for spelling errors. You'll write the correct spellings on the blanks.

Lesson 112

Grammar

1. In your workbook is another practice with plurals vs. possessives.
2. Look back at the directions for Lesson 104 if you want a reminder.

Lesson 113

Writing

1. You are going to write for ten minutes on ANY topic. You could write about what you did yesterday or your favorite thing to do.
2. Don't start the timer until you have your first sentence written.

Lesson 114

Grammar

1. Complete your worksheet page for today.
2. There is another possessives/plurals practice.

Lesson 115

Writing

1. You are going to write for ten minutes on ANY topic. You could write about what you are going to do this weekend or a place you'd like to go.
2. Don't start the timer until you have your first sentence written.

Lesson 116

Grammar

1. Complete the activity practicing possessives vs. plurals.
2. You can check back to Lesson 104 if you need a reminder.

Lesson 117

Writing

1. You are going to write a point of view story. Actually, two. Actually, one.
2. You are going to write a short story, a page or less. You will write the same story two times, each time from a different point of view. Each time your "I" will be a different character in the story.
3. Your story could have two people who experience the same day but one is having a good and one a bad day.

4. You could write about Paul Revere's ride and one character could be Paul Revere and the other character could be his horse.
5. Be creative. See how different you can make the two stories while keeping them the *same story*.
6. Today come up with your plan. Know what your story is going to be. Describe your two characters and how the story will differ. You can use your workbook page for this.

Lesson 118
Writing
1. Write your first story.
2. There is no workbook page for this. It would be best to type it to make editing easier.

Lesson 119
Writing
1. Write your second story.
2. There is no workbook page for this. Type it if you can.

Lesson 120
Writing
1. Finish your stories. Edit them thoroughly.
2. Make sure you have varied types of sentences and sentence lengths. Make sure you have at least one simile or metaphor. Make sure you use good descriptive words, strong verbs, and specific nouns.
3. Check your capitalization and punctuation.
4. Read your stories aloud to an audience.
5. Add your name, date, and titles ("Point of View 1" and "Point of View 2") to them and print them out. Give them to a parent to add to your portfolio.

Lesson 121
Spelling
1. Have someone read your spelling words from the Lesson 121 answer page in the back of the Lesson Guide. Write them as best as you can.
2. Check them and write correctly any that were misspelled.
3. Figure out why you wrote what you did and how you can remember the correct way, maybe by pronouncing the word a little differently.
4. Then try writing those corrected words again without looking.

Lesson 122
Spelling
1. Work on your spelling.
2. This unscramble uses the words from Lesson 121, so you can peek back if necessary.
3. The point is to pay attention to how they are spelled.
4. When your work is checked, make sure the spelling of each word is checked.
5. Rewrite any that were spelled wrong; don't only fix them.

Lesson 123

Spelling

1. Fill in the blanks.
2. Again, these are the same spelling words, so you can look back IF you can't figure out a word.
3. When your work is checked, make sure the spelling of each word is checked.
4. Rewrite any that were spelled wrong; don't only fix them.

Lesson 124

Spelling

1. Play hangman. Have someone play with you.
   - They will find the word to use for Lesson 124 in the answer key.
   - They will tell you how many letters are in the word. Draw that number of blanks on a piece of paper.
   - Guess one letter at a time. If the letter is in the word, have them tell you which blank or blanks it goes in. Write it in.
   - If you want, for each wrong guess, draw a piece of a picture. Try to guess the word before you finish your picture.
2. This one should be done without looking back!

Lesson 125

Spelling

1. Take the spelling test. Have someone read the words to you from the answer key.
2. Any word you spell incorrectly today, rewrite five times, correctly of course.

Lesson 126

Spelling

1. Have someone read your spelling words from the Lesson 126 answer page in the back of the Lesson Guide. Write them as best as you can.
2. Check them and write correctly any that were misspelled.
3. Figure out why you wrote what you did and how you can remember the correct way, maybe by pronouncing the word a little differently.
4. Then try writing those corrected words again without looking.

Lesson 127

Spelling

1. Work on your spelling.
2. This unscramble uses the words from Lesson 6, so you can peek back if necessary.
3. The point is to pay attention to how they are spelled.
4. When your work is checked, make sure the spelling of each word is checked.
5. Rewrite any that were spelled wrong; don't only fix them.

Lesson 128

Spelling

1. Fill in the blanks.
2. Again, these are the same spelling words, so you can look back IF you can't figure out a word.
3. When your work is checked, make sure the spelling of each word is checked.
4. Rewrite any that were spelled wrong; don't only fix them.

Lesson 129

Spelling

1. Play hangman. Have someone play with you.
   - They will find the word to use for Lesson 129 in the answer key.
   - They will tell you how many letters are in the word. Draw that number of blanks on a piece of paper.
   - Guess one letter at a time. If the letter is in the word, have them tell you which blank or blanks it goes in. Write it in.
   - If you want, for each wrong guess, draw a piece of a picture. Try to guess the word before you finish your picture.
2. This one should be done without looking back!

Lesson 130

Spelling

1. Take the spelling test. Have someone read the words to you from the answer key.
2. Any word you spell incorrectly today, rewrite five times, correctly of course.

Lesson 131

Grammar

1. There is one more type of phrase I want you to learn. I think it's the easiest. You've learned gerunds, participles, and now **infinitives**. The **infinitive** of a verb is when it is combined with "to." *To eat dinner* is an infinitive phrase. We're headed home *to eat dinner*. The "to" goes next to the verb, otherwise you have "split the infinitive."
   - To the verb is a prepositional phrase, not an infinitive phrase. An infinitive phrase is "to" plus a verb.
2. Find the infinitive phrases on the workbook page for today.

Lesson 132

Spelling

1. Complete the word search in your workbook.

Lesson 133

Spelling

1. Do you remember your spelling words?
2. Have someone read the words that belong in the blanks using the answer key.

Lesson 134

Grammar

1. Do the workbook activity on gerunds and infinitives.
2. Write in the infinitive form or the gerund form (e.g. to read or reading).

Lesson 135

Writing

1. Write a song.
2. It can be short. It can be just a chorus.

Lesson 136

Writing

1. Write one of each type of sentence.
   - declarative, interrogative, exclamatory, imperative, simple, compound, complex, using "however," using a semicolon
2. Get a high five and/or hug if you put them all into a story instead of writing isolated sentences.

Lesson 137

Grammar

1. Complete the activity on participle phrases and dangling modifiers.
2. The word after the comma must be what is being modified. You can reword the sentence or move the modifier to make the sentence correct.
   - Bounding into the house, the dog left muddy tracks. "The dog" comes after the comma. It is what bounding into the house is referring to. You couldn't write: Bounding into the house, muddy tracks were everywhere. Bounding does not describe muddy tracks. It describes the dog.

Lesson 138

Grammar

1. Do the workbook exercise on participle phrases and dangling modifiers.
2. You are looking for the correct sentence.

Lesson 139

Grammar

1. Try another exercise on misused modifiers in your workbook today.
2. You'll be reading a story and working to spot them.

Lesson 140

Writing

1. There's a creative writing activity for you today.
2. If you could heal 12 people, and only 12, who would you heal and why?

Lesson 141

Spelling
1. Find the misspelled words in the paragraph on your workbook page today.
2. Here's a little spelling point. The prefix AD- means to or toward. With many words, when combined, the D is dropped and the beginning consonant is doubled. Here are some examples of AD words.
    - advertise
    - acclaim
    - adopt
    - affix
    - adhere
    - allocate
    - accomplish
    - associate

Lesson 142

7th Grade Test
1. Complete the reading comprehension activity in your workbook.

Lesson 143

7th Grade Test
1. Complete the reading comprehension activity in your workbook.

Lesson 144

7th Grade Test
1. Complete the reading comprehension activity in your workbook.

Lesson 145

7th Grade Test
1. Complete the reading comprehension activity in your workbook.

Lesson 146

7th Grade Test
1. Complete the reading comprehension activity in your workbook.

Lesson 147

7th Grade Test
1. Complete the reading comprehension activity in your workbook.

Lesson 148

7th Grade Test
1. Complete the reading comprehension activity in your workbook.

Lesson 149

7th Grade Test
1. Complete the reading comprehension activity in your workbook.

Lesson 150

7th Grade Test

1. Complete the reading comprehension activity in your workbook.

Lesson 151

Spelling

1. Find and correct the five misspelled words in the paragraph.
2. Spelling review: long vowels
    1. a --> ai, ay, a_e
    2. e --> e, y, ie, ee, ea, i_e, e_e
    3. i --> igh, y, i_e
    4. u--> ue, eu, ew, u_e
    5. o--> ow, ough, oe, o_e
3. Can you think of an example of each spelling?

Lesson 152

Writing

1. Complete the metaphor and genre worksheets. There are two pages for today.
2. You are going to be writing your own novel. Today, choose your book's genre.

Lesson 153

Writing

1. Do the sentence structure worksheet in your workbook.
2. Every story has a **protagonist,** the main character, our hero. Every story exists in the **conflict** between the protagonist and the antagonist.
3. The **antagonist** doesn't have to be the "bad guy." It could be the weather or terrain in a story about pioneers traveling west.
4. There must be **conflict** or you have no story.
5. Decide on your main characters. You need a **protagonist and antagonist.**
6. Describe them in as much detail as possible using the second workbook page for today.
    - You should be able to picture them.
    - You should know their strengths and weaknesses; they should both have both.
    - Do they have a bad habit? Something they say all the time?
    - Are they funny, serious, a loner, a friend to everyone?

Lesson 154

Writing

1. You should be thinking about your story. You should know your **antagonist and protagonist**. You should know what **conflict** will arise between them.
2. If you are reading *The King Will Make a Way,* what's the conflict?
3. There needs to be an incident in the beginning of your novel that sets off the conflict.
4. If you are reading *The King Will Make a Way,* what sets off the conflict?
5. The beginning of your novel needs to pose a question that's not going to be answered until the end.
6. If you are reading *The King Will Make a Way,* what's the question?

7. Use your workbook to answer these questions: What will set off your story? What is the big question in your book? What is the answer going to be?
   Answers: #2 Vulpine wants the king dead so he can rule. Gabe knows the King is alive, and he wants Him to rule the village. #4 Gabe reads the Book of Law which makes him believe the King is alive. #6 Who will be king of the village?

Lesson 155
Writing
1. I'm trying to get you started on your novel as soon as possible, but we need to visit characters one more time.
2. Consider giving your protagonist and antagonist each a sidekick, a best friend, a helper, a tag-along-er.
3. If you are reading *The King Will Make a Way,* who is Gabe's "sidekick"? Who is Vulpine's "sidekick"?
4. Choose your supporting characters. Describe them in detail just like your main characters using the workbook pages. You should be able to draw a picture of them. You should know just what they look like and act like. What are their strengths and weaknesses? Quirks? Personalities?
5. Be thinking about your story. How is it going to begin? What's it going to be called? How is it going to end?
6. Do the descriptive writing assignment in your workbook.
7. Write your descriptions. Read them to someone and see if they know what you are describing.
   Answers: #3 Angela, Phineas

Lesson 156
Writing
1. You have characters. They are in conflict. Your story is set up, but…
2. Where is it going to take place?
3. You need to decide on your setting, the time and place of your story. You need a main setting. Is it in the future? present day? historical? Is it at your house, in your town, in India, in outer space, in a fictional land?
4. Write a description using your workbook page for today. Draw a picture. Know everything about your setting.
5. There is a second worksheet to complete on types of sentences.

Lesson 157
Writing
1. Today write descriptions for different minor settings in your novel: a room, a field, a tree house, a ship…
2. Add as many details as possible. Picture it. The more details, the better your book will be.
3. What about those locations will help or hinder your protagonist, your antagonist?
4. Is there a secret hiding spot somewhere? Is there an object lying around there that will help out one of your characters?
5. There is a second page in your workbook as well, on parallel sentences. There are examples on the page.

Lesson 158

Writing

1. On your worksheet for today, make a list of five objects that you could put into your story. If you get stuck, go back and look at the list and maybe you'll get an idea.
2. Make a list of complications that could arise for your protagonist and for your antagonist.
3. If everything went right all the time for your protagonist, it would be boring. There have to be ups and downs. It has to look like the answer to your question will yes, then no, then yes, then no. It's not going to be an exciting conclusion unless it seems impossible.

Lesson 159

Writing

1. Your story will start with the "exposition." That's the background of the story. It sets the scene.
2. Then there will be an incident that sets of the action of the story and raises the big question.
3. Then there is the conflict, the action as the story progresses. This is called the "rising action."
4. Then you are going to get to the exciting part, the climax. The answer to the question hangs in the balance. We are in suspense. What's going to happen? This can play out over a few chapters.
5. Then the answer comes. This is the "falling action."
6. Then the end comes, the "resolution." We find out what happens to everyone and we end with a good, happy, warm and fuzzy feeling.
7. Write out each of these steps for your story using the workbook page for today.

Lesson 160

Writing

1. Make a list of chapter titles on your workbook page today.
2. Each chapter is its own little story.
3. Old fashioned books used to have as chapter titles such as "In Which Winnie the Pooh Gets Stuck in a Jar of Honey."
4. Write titles like that. You don't have to use them in the book. It's like making an outline.
5. You need to set the background, set off your story, have conflict and complications, ups and downs, set up your climax, have lots of excitement and tension, answer the question, tie everything up with a neat, pretty bow.

Lesson 161

Writing

1. Read the lesson below and do the worksheet on oxymoron and irony.
   - *Ironically, to accomplish this peace Vulpine turned to General Writ.*
   - Irony is when something is the opposite of what it should be. In the sentence above the irony is that he wants peace, but he's going to fight.
   - I remember seeing a political cartoon full of irony. The pro-lifer says, "Killing is wrong," but he kills the abortion doctor. Then the judge says, "Killing is wrong," but he gives the pro-lifer the death sentence. See the irony? They say killing is wrong, but they do the opposite, they kill.

- *The troops marched behind their subordinate leader toward the hill.*
- An oxymoron is another use of opposites. It is when two contradictory terms are used together: her cruel kindness, in slow haste, and in this case "subordinate leader," or the leader who is under authority. Do you see how each of these terms is an oxymoron?
    - act naturally, open secret, only choice, alone together, tragic comedy
2. Often books use **foreshadowing**. It tells you something that is going to happen. Foreshadowing makes you curious about what's going to happen. It often makes you say, "What!? Why?"
3. You can use it at the end of a chapter to get your audience to turn the page and read on!
4. If you are reading *The King Will Make a Way,* find an example of foreshadowing on the *first* page of chapter 9.
5. Look over your descriptions and everything you've written in preparation.
6. Now get started. Write at least your first page. Getting started is the hardest. Once you start, keep up the momentum and keep going!

Answers: foreshadow example: "unaware he would never again climb the hill to meet the King" Did it make you take notice and wonder what was going to happen?

Lesson 162
Writing
1. Write. Write for at least thirty minutes.
2. Don't get stuck. Just keep writing. You can always edit it later.

Lesson 163
Writing
1. When you write, picture your story in your mind. It should play like a movie in your mind.
2. Read the dialog lesson below and then complete the worksheet for today and dialog writing assignment, or write a dialog in your novel.
    - The first example:
        - "Our spies tell us that in the morning Vulpine will condescend to be among the common folk," Stone mocked.
        - "Stone mocked" is a speech tag.
        - A speech tag is the most common way to write dialog.
        - This type of tag is preceded by a comma.
        - If you were telling this to someone you would say, "Stone mocked that our spies…"
        - If you were telling someone a story, you wouldn't say, It's number five. He said.
        - You would say, He said it was number five.
        - You can see how this type of tag is part of the sentence.
        - The comma (instead of a period) keeps it as part of the sentence.
        - By the way, if it was a question or exclamation, you would keep those punctuation marks.
        - "He said what?" she asked again. (Notice the lower case she…remember it's all part of the same sentence.)

- A second example:
  - "They are greedy for money and power and despise virtue." Stone rose and began methodically pacing the length of the room.
  - This quote is followed by an action tag. It's not a he said, she said tag. It's describing what the character did.
  - This type of tag is preceded by a period, or question mark, or exclamation point. It is its own sentence.
  - You could also tell who's speaking by using a descriptive tag. This is also its own sentence and does not use the comma like a speech tag.
  - Rachel's eyes were shining. "I'll be there."
  - A speech tag would look like this: Rachel's eyes were shining when she told her, "I'll be there."
- A third example:

  "The imposter Vulpine surely is cunning, but his arrogance has led him to believe he can control us with bribes and fancy words. He thinks too highly of his own power.

  "I offer to you that this is his blind spot."
  - This example is showing the end of one paragraph and the beginning of another. Both are Stone speaking. The one paragraph ends with him saying "his own power" and the next begins with him saying, "I offer to you…."
  - Did you notice the lack of quotation mark after power?
  - When a long quotation transitions from one paragraph to another, you don't close the quotation at the end of the paragraph, but you open the new paragraph with a quotation mark to show the character is still talking.
- Since I've already gone onto a second page, let me take the opportunity to write some things about writing dialog.

  1. The dialog should be important to the story to move the story along.

  2. The reader needs to know who's talking, but if two people are talking back and forth, you don't need to label each sentence with a tag.

  3. Vary the types of tags you use—speech tag, action tag, descriptive tag.

  4. If the character said it, then use "he said." Getting too creative in ways to say "say" is a distraction. If the character whispered, then use whisper. If the character mumbled, then use mumble. But don't just throw in words for said from the thesaurus to break up the monotony of he said, she said. Use action tags and descriptive tags instead.

  5. And one last rule, each time the speaker changes, you need to start a new paragraph.

Lesson 164
Writing
1. When you write dialog, make sure the dialog plays a part in story. It shouldn't be meaningless. It should reveal to us more about the characters or move the story along.
2. Read the lesson below and complete the uncommon punctuation lesson in your workbook. Do the free-writing at the bottom of the page or do it as part of your novel.

- From the book: *He knew of their meetings and their disloyalty, but they were a bunch of weaklings: women, children and old men, only a few straggly others joined them. There were the rooks, his guards; the queen, his devoted servants whom he could bid come to his side at a moment's notice; and he, of course, was the king. That left the knights, those horses that fancied themselves special—the only pieces on a chess board allowed to jump over another.*
- We're not going to discuss common comma rules. Let's look at some trickier punctuation. Each of the sentences above (from a paragraph in chapter 12) has a special form of punctuation.
- Let's start with the first.
    - Sentence 1: Find the colon. What purpose does it serve? It sets off a list.
    - Sentence 2: Find the two semi-colons. What purpose do they serve? They act as commas in a list. They are used because a comma is needed inside the items in the list.
        - If I wrote, "Call Amy, Mary, the one from co-op, Chris, Martha, and Stacy." It looks like "the one from co-op" is someone on the list. If I really am trying to tell you which Mary to call, then I need to use semi-colons. "Call Amy; Mary, the one from co-op; Chris; Martha; and Stacy."
    - Sentence 3: Find the dash. What purpose does it serve? It acts almost like a parenthesis. You are saying something separate, off to the side. Do you see how the dash in that sentence serves that purpose?

Lesson 165
Writing
1. Write, write, write!
2. Read the lesson on metaphor and complete the worksheet page for today. If you aren't reading *The King Will Make a Way*, find any metaphor example in a book you are reading or have recently read for school or just write your own example.
    - Remember, a metaphor is where one thing is said to be another.
    - A metaphor doesn't have to include both things that are being compared.
    - In chapter five we read: *A heavy fist was pounding the roof, and the three tried to ignore the percussion symphony playing for them outside, especially the hail which was using the inn as a kettle drum.*
        - I don't say that the fist is the hail hitting the roof. I don't say that the "percussion symphony" is all the crashing of things outside. But the reader understands the comparison.
    - Here is another example of an extended metaphor. *Standing by the village well, Vulpine's senses were on high alert as he detected a change of tone in the harmony of the village. He was certain he discerned discord among the villagers. Phineas had made an announcement and not everyone was parroting his words. When they did, it was a beautiful melody to Vulpine. Now a sour note was written into the strain. Insistent on rooting it out, he directed his spies to report on all village activity and discourse. By moonrise he had his finger on the key. It was the King.* (chapter 10)
        - This is an extended music metaphor and really a play on musical words.

- The musical words in here are: tone, harmony, discord, melody, sour note, strain, key. There is no actual strain of music with a sour note written into it. People repeating what Vulpine says isn't really a melody.

Lesson 166
Writing
1. Do the anthropomorphism worksheet in your workbook. Either do the writing portion or write it into your novel.
2. Write, write, write!

Lesson 167
Writing
1. Read the lesson on lie vs. lay and complete the worksheet.
   - Here's a piece of grammar that tripped me up when I wrote my first draft—the past tense of the verb to lie. Let's start with the present tense. We have to lie and to lay.
   - Which one is which? The easiest distinction is that lie is what you do to yourself and lay is what you do to something else.
     - You lie down to take a nap. You lay the paper on the table.
     - My baby lies down for a nap. I lay my baby down for his nap.
   - Let's move on to the past tense. This is where I tripped up.
   - I lie down for a nap every afternoon. Yesterday I lay down for a nap in the afternoon. I have lain down for an afternoon nap every afternoon this week.
   - I lay out the kids' school books every morning. Yesterday I laid out the kids' school books in the morning. I have laid out the kids' school books every morning this week.
   - Example from the book (chapter 14): *Before they could worry about how he was to mount her, she lay down. They helped their father onto her back and laid him down against her mane.*
     - Do you see both types here? The horse lies down herself, and Gabe and Angela lay their father down.
     - Of course, it looks different here because it is in the past tense.
       - Lie in the past is lay.
       - Lay in the past is laid.
2. Write, write, and write some more.

Lesson 168
Writing
1. Write for 30 minutes.
2. Have you finished your book too soon? Add more problems! More excitement!

Lesson 169
Writing
1. Spend 30 minutes writing.

Lesson 170

Writing

1. STOP! Go back and read your story out loud. Picture it as a movie in your mind. Hear the characters talk. Change anything that doesn't flow or make sense. Have you used all of your characters' characteristics? What is it they say all the time? Are they acting shy, funny, etc.? Have you shown their bad habits and other weaknesses? Have you described the setting so that everyone will picture the same thing?

2. Do some editing today before you move on.

Lesson 171

Writing

1. Read the personification lesson for chapter 20. If you write personification into your book today, you can skip writing your own examples on the worksheet.
   - Here are examples of personification from *The King Will Make a Way*.
     - The word permanent landed heavy in the middle of the room. (ch. 20)
     - ...the thirsty flames licked up the water as soon as it was poured out. (ch. 14)
     - It hissed and spat as the oil and water quarreled. (ch. 7)
   - Personification is when something inanimate is described as if it were animate.
   - Some other examples are:
     - Like my new car? She's a real beauty.
     - The chair groaned under his weight.
     - The angry river raged through the valley.
   - In the examples from the book…
     - The word permanent is said to have landed and to be heavy.
     - The flames are described as being thirsty and licking.
     - The oil and water are described as quarreling.

2. Write for 30 minutes.

Lesson 172

Writing

1. Write for thirty minutes.

Lesson 173

Writing

1. Write for thirty minutes.

Lesson 174

Writing

1. Write for thirty minutes.

Lesson 175

Writing

1. Write for thirty minutes.

Lesson 176
Writing
1. Write for thirty minutes.

Lesson 177
Writing
1. Where are you in your novel? Have you figured out how to set up your climax? How it is all going to play out and resolve?
2. Keep writing.
3. Read about alliteration and complete your worksheet. You can leave any lines blank that you put into your novel instead. Don't forget to make longer ones.
    - bouncing, burping baby boy
    - From chapter 12 ...or does the dastardly devil deserve to die?

Lesson 178
Writing
1. Do the worksheet page on onomatopoeia. You don't have to do the writing page if you add onomatopoeia into your novel today.
2. Write for 30 minutes.

Lesson 179
Writing
1. Read your novel. Make sure you are watching the movie of your book in your mind. What needs changing? What doesn't make sense? What doesn't sound right? What needs more description? How can you add longer sentences, similes, metaphors, foreshadowing.
2. Keep writing.

Lesson 180
Writing
1. You made it to the last day of school. I don't know where you are in your novel.
2. Keep writing if you have more to go.
3. If you got to the end, spend lots of time reading your novel and making it better. Writers spend as much time editing as they do writing.
4. Choose better words. Change the lengths of your sentences. Add to your descriptions.
5. Ask others to read it and where they have questions add more in to make it clear to your audience.
6. If you want to turn it into a real book, you can use a free service through Amazon.com. Follow their directions and you can publish your book for free. It will help you make a cover and everything. Then your friends and family can buy your book!

EP Language Arts 7

Workbook Answers

Lesson 6

Lesson 6: Spelling

See how many words you can spell correctly the first time as they are read to you. Learn from any mistakes you make.

abbreviation	absolutely
absorb	accessible
achievement	acres
adjustable	admittance
advice	advise
afghan	analysis
analyze	artificial
assistance	association
attendance	authority

Lesson 7

Lesson 7: Spelling - Unscramble

EIRAIBVAOTBN	abbreviation
AEULDTSBAJ	adjustable
OABRBS	absorb
SOOTASIICNA	association
BCSLICEESA	accessible
CEAANDENTT	attendance
TAVNIEHECEM	achievement
TNTMIACDEA	admittance
ALLBOUYSET	absolutely
RSCAE	acres
YZANELA	analyze
HAFGNA	afghan
SASNLYAI	analysis
HAIURTOTY	authority
CLIIARATIF	artificial
DVESAI	advise
NCSIAAESST	assistance
VCDEIA	advice

Lesson 8

Lesson 8: Spelling

The park included three __acres__ of luscious grass.

The seatbelt was __adjustable__ to fit her small waist.

I would __advise__ against speaking disrespectfully.

The __afghan__ kept her warm when the heat went out.

What's your __analysis__ of this situation?

This __artificial__ sweetener has an aftertaste.

Are you __absolutely__ certain you turned off the stove?

What has been your greatest __achievement__ this year?

The sign said, "No __admittance__."

Can you offer your __assistance__ to that lady?

What's the postal __abbreviation__ for Massachusetts?

Do you submit to those in __authority__?

Her __attendance__ at the meetings was sporadic at best.

The sponge will __absorb__ the entire spill.

What's your __advice__ on this topic?

The playground was __accessible__ to all kids.

When I __analyze__ the budget, I see a deficit.

I have a close __association__ with my co-worker.

Lesson 9

Lesson 9: Spelling - Hangman

Play hangman! See if you can figure out your spelling words in ten guesses or less. Cross out letters you've guessed to help yourself keep track. The words are in the Lesson Guide.

A B C D E F G H I J K L M N O P Q R S T U V W X Y Z

a   b   s   o   r   b

A B C D E F G H I J K L M N O P Q R S T U V W X Y Z

a   c   r   e   s

A B C D E F G H I J K L M N O P Q R S T U V W X Y Z

a   d   v   i   c   e

A B C D E F G H I J K L M N O P Q R S T U V W X Y Z

a   d   v   i   s   e

A B C D E F G H I J K L M N O P Q R S T U V W X Y Z

a   f   g   h   a   n

A B C D E F G H I J K L M N O P Q R S T U V W X Y Z

a   n   a   l   y   z   e

Lesson 10

Lesson 10: Spelling
Language Arts 7

See how many words you can spell correctly the first time as they are read to you. Learn from any mistakes you make.

abbreviation	absolutely
absorb	accessible
achievement	acres
adjustable	admittance
advice	advise
afghan	analysis
analyze	artificial
assistance	association
attendance	authority

Lesson 11

Lesson 11: Spelling
Language Arts 7

See how many words you can spell correctly the first time as they are read to you. Learn from any mistakes you make.

bacteria	bagel
bicycle	biscuit
bizarre	boulevard
boundary	bouquet
bureau	campaign
capital	capitol
cinnamon	commotion
competition	confetti
congratulations	culprit

Lesson 12

Lesson 12: Spelling - Unscramble
Language Arts 7

TBUEOQU	bouquet
ETRACAIB	bacteria
PTAALIC	capital
ALGEB	bagel
UEBRUA	bureau
CEYLICB	bicycle
ANINMONC	cinnamon
DBUOVEARL	boulevard
PMGNIACA	campaign
NODBRUAY	boundary
TNOECFTI	confetti
ICPOLTA	capitol
EIMINCTTOPO	competition
TILUCPR	culprit
SIBTCUI	biscuit
NMOITMCOO	commotion
NAOALGCIONUTSTR	congratulations
RBAIREZ	bizarre

Lesson 13

Lesson 13: Spelling
Language Arts 7

Iris picked a lovely __bouquet__ of wildflowers.

__Congratulations__ are in order for the winners.

The state __capitol__ building is located downtown.

The infection in my throat was caused by __bacteria__.

Do you put __cinnamon__ on your applesauce?

The presidential __campaign__ was successful.

I rode my __bicycle__ to work yesterday.

The __bizarre__ comment left me scratching my head.

What's all the __commotion__ outside?

The bushes form a natural __boundary__ for the property.

Do you like cream cheese on your __bagel__?

The __boulevard__ winds its way by the beautiful park.

The crowd threw __confetti__ as the newlyweds ran past.

The __capital__ of California is Sacramento.

Chase likes to put honey on his morning __biscuit__.

Sara put her jewelry box on top of the __bureau__.

It seems a mouse was the cookie thief __culprit__.

The __competition__ was fierce at the spelling bee.

Lesson 14

Lesson 14: Spelling - Hangman

Play hangman! See if you can figure out your spelling words in ten guesses or less. Cross out letters you've guessed to help yourself keep track. The words are in the Lesson Guide.

A B C D E F G H I J K L M N O P Q R S T U V W X Y Z

b u r e a u

A B C D E F G H I J K L M N O P Q R S T U V W X Y Z

c u l p r i t .

A B C D E F G H I J K L M N O P Q R S T U V W X Y Z

c a m p a i g n .

A B C D E F G H I J K L M N O P Q R S T U V W X Y Z

b i c y c l e

A B C D E F G H I J K L M N O P Q R S T U V W X Y Z

c o n f e t t i .

A B C D E F G H I J K L M N O P Q R S T U V W X Y Z

b i s c u i t

Lesson 15

Lesson 15: Spelling

See how many words you can spell correctly the first time as they are read to you. Learn from any mistakes you make.

bacteria	bagel
bicycle	biscuit
bizarre	boulevard
boundary	bouquet
bureau	campaign
capital	capitol
cinnamon	commotion
competition	confetti
congratulations	culprit

Lesson 16

Lesson 16: Spelling

See how many words you can spell correctly the first time as they are read to you. Learn from any mistakes you make.

deceive	delayed
democracy	deodorant
description	diameter
dismissal	distinguished
embarrass	emphasize
encircle	engineer
evident	exhibit
extinct	extinguish
extraordinary	extremely

Lesson 17

Lesson 17: Spelling - Unscramble

TDEDOONRA	deodorant
IENTEDV	evident
EIHSMEAPZ	emphasize
AISSISDML	dismissal
EEICDEV	deceive
MRSERBAAS	embarrass
YRMEETELX	extremely
YDDLEAE	delayed
XIETIBH	exhibit
NRCECLIE	encircle
ENAROXADRYRTI	extraordinary
EIAMTDRE	diameter
OREACCYDM	democracy
XHUIEINSGT	extinguish
CNTEXTI	extinct
ERGEINEN	engineer
SIGUEIDDTNHSI	distinguished
ERINCDPOITS	description

Lesson 18

Lesson 18: Spelling

The art __exhibit__ at the museum was a great field trip.

The incoming snow led to the meeting's __dismissal__ .

Our __distinguished__ guest was the mayor.

Not to __embarrass__ you, but there's lettuce in your teeth.

The item's __description__ said it was brand new.

The project __engineer__ said the build was on schedule.

The firemen worked hard to __extinguish__ the flame.

The __diameter__ of the hoop was smaller than the ball.

The species was nearly __extinct__ , but made a comeback.

I wasn't trying to __deceive__ , it was just a surprise.

The ants began to __encircle__ the crumbs.

The race is __delayed__ due to rain.

Is __democracy__ a good system of government?

It is __evident__ to me that God exists.

You don't need to yell to __emphasize__ your point.

The firework display was __extraordinary__ !

This __deodorant__ has way too strong of a scent for me.

She is __extremely__ tired after her long weekend.

Lesson 19

Lesson 19: Spelling - Hangman

Play hangman! See if you can figure out your spelling words in ten guesses or less. Cross out letters you've guessed to help yourself keep track. The words are in the Lesson Guide.

A B C D E F G H I J K L M N O P Q R S T U V W X Y Z

e x h i b i t

A B C D E F G H I J K L M N O P Q R S T U V W X Y Z

d e l a y e d

A B C D E F G H I J K L M N O P Q R S T U V W X Y Z

e n c i r c l e

A B C D E F G H I J K L M N O P Q R S T U V W X Y Z

e x t i n c t

A B C D E F G H I J K L M N O P Q R S T U V W X Y Z

e v i d e n t

A B C D E F G H I J K L M N O P Q R S T U V W X Y Z

d e c e i v e

Lesson 20

Lesson 20: Spelling

See how many words you can spell correctly the first time as they are read to you. Learn from any mistakes you make.

deceive	delayed
democracy	deodorant
description	diameter
dismissal	distinguished
embarrass	emphasize
encircle	engineer
evident	exhibit
extinct	extinguish
extraordinary	extremely

Lesson 21

Lesson 21: Spelling

Fill in this crossword using the spelling words listed at the bottom. These are words from the spelling lists from lessons 6, 11, and 16.

absorb	bacteria	deceive
advice	biscuit	diameter
advise	bureau	encircle
analyze	commotion	evident
artificial	confetti	exhibit
authority	congratulations	

Crossword answers:
COMMOTION, ENCIRCLE, CONGRATULATIONS, ABSORB, ARTIFICIAL, ADVICE, EXHIBIT, BUREAU, ANALYZE, DECEIVE, ADVISE, CONFETTI, BACTERIA, AUTHORITY

Lesson 22

Lesson 22: Proofreading

Spelling corrections are bold, punctuation marks are circled, and capitalization errors are underlined.

Marie Curie, or Madame Curie as she is known to many, was a scientist in the late 19th and early 20th **centuries.** Born in Poland, she moved to France to continue her scientific studies and ended up marrying a physics professor. The **pair** worked together for the advancement of science, particularly physics.

Marie Curie shattered glass ceilings all over the place. She co-earned a Nobel Prize in 1903, making her the first woman ever to earn **one.** She went on to earn another one as well. After her husband's death, she took his place as professor of physics. She was the first **woman** to hold the position.

Madame Curie is most known for her work with radium. Although exposure to the element eventually killed her, her research **led** to advancements in x-ray machines, which improve lives daily, almost a century after her death.

Lesson 23

Lesson 23: Proofreading

Spelling corrections are bold, punctuation marks are circled, and capitalization errors are underlined.

At the end of World War II, Germany, as well as its former capital of <u>Berlin</u>, was divided between the Allies and Russia. In the post-war period, many people emigrated from the Russian side of East Germany **to** help rebuild the Allies' West Germany. The economy of East Germany suffered greatly from the lack of labor. In order to keep people from emigrating, as well as to protect their communist society from Western influence, East Germany built a guarded brick wall in 1961 and topped it with barbed wire.

The wall was an immediate publicity catastrophe for East Germany and communism as a **whole.** The wall itself, along with the very public punishments of those who tried to cross it, showcased the tyranny of communism. Under U.S. pressure, the wall came down on November 9, 1989, and within three years, all but three communist nations had collapsed.

Lesson 24

Lesson 24: Proofreading

Spelling corrections are bold, punctuation marks are circled, and capitalization errors are underlined.

Jesse Owens was the grandson of a slave. Born in September of 1913 in Alabama, Jesse was the youngest of ten children. Along with 1.5 million other <u>African American</u>s who were part of the "Great Migration," his family left the segregated <u>South</u> when he was nine years old and moved to Ohio in search of better opportunities. It was in Ohio that Jesse became a track and field star.

He was only in high school when he gained national attention for tying the world record in the 100 yard dash. At a college track **meet,** it took him less than an hour's time to break three world records and tie a **fourth.** Then at the 1936 Olympics, Jesse Owens achieved a feat no Olympian had ever achieved up to that point when he earned four gold medals. Jesse's performance undermined Adolf Hitler's ridiculous claims about racial superiority.

Lesson 27

Lesson 27: Proofreading

Spelling corrections are bold, and punctuation marks are circled.

Philip Sousa was born in Washington, D.C., the third of ten children. When he was thirteen, his father enlisted him in the Marine Corps **to** keep him from joining a circus band. He started as an apprentice with the Marine Band, and then he moved on **to** a theatrical orchestra where he learned to conduct. He then returned to the Marine Band as a conductor, going on to lead "The President's Band" under five presidents.

Sousa went on to be a composer of marches, earning him the nickname "the American March King." His most famous marches include the following: the U.S. National March called "The Stars and Stripes Forever" and "Semper Fidelis," the **official** march of the U.S. Marine Corps. He eventually conducted his own band, named the Sousa Band, which featured a new instrument that most every marching band today uses – the aptly named sousaphone.

Lesson 29

Lesson 29: Proofreading • Grammar

Spelling corrections are bold, punctuation marks are circled, and capitalization errors are underlined.

Clive Staples Lewis is a well-known British author, most famous **for** his *Chronicles of Narnia* series of books. **Though** his Christian faith is evident throughout many of his writings⊙ C.S. Lewis actually left Christianity for atheism during his university years. However⊙ after years of intellectual wrestling⊙ Lewis returned to Christianity and became a great defender of the faith.

Identify the part of speech of the underlined word by writing it on the line.

That <u>jump</u> was the highest of the meet.   noun

I'll let <u>myself</u> out.   pronoun

I'd love to fly <u>among</u> the stars.   preposition

The <u>shining</u> sun blinded the driver.   adjective

That fruit salad <u>looks</u> delicious!   verb

We're <u>very</u> late for the meeting!   adverb

Lesson 30

Lesson 30: Proofreading

Spelling corrections are bold, and punctuation marks are circled.

Leonardo da Vinci **might** be one of the most underrated people in history. You probably know he was an artist⊙ particularly a painter and **sculptor**. But he excelled in many other areas as well. He was a scientist who specialized in anatomy⊙ geology⊙ and botany⊙ He was also a **writer**, a mathematician, a musician, an architect, an engineer, a cartographer, and an impressive inventor.

Da Vinci's inventions were amazingly ahead of his **time**. He invented the predecessor to the modern-day tank centuries before cars were invented. He even invented a fully animated robot while living in the 1400s! But his most famous invention stemmed from his favorite area of study — aviation. His famous flying machine probably **had** his Renaissance neighbors thinking he was as batty as the winged night creatures he studied to design it!

Lesson 32

Lesson 32: Proofreading

Spelling corrections are bold, punctuation marks are circled, and capitalization errors are underlined.

Mary Elizabeth Bowser was a slave during the 1800✗s. As a young woman, she was freed by her owner and sent to a Quaker school where she learned to read and **write**. Once the <u>Civil War</u> began⊙ her kind, former owner asked if she would help the <u>union</u> by spying on the Confederacy.

To do this, Mary had to pretend to be dim-witted and uneducated. She also had to go back to being treated like a slave, a life she had largely gotten **away** from. She was hired by Jefferson Davis, the president of the Confederacy. Using her position within his home, she would eavesdrop on conversations⊙ read private communication✗s⊙ and then relay the information to a fellow spy who posed as a baker making regular bread deliveries. More than 100 years later, Mary was inducted into the U.S. Army Military Intelligence Corps Hall of Fame for her efforts.

Lesson 33

Lesson 33: Proofreading

Spelling corrections are bold, punctuation marks are circled, and capitalization errors are underlined.

James Weldon Johnson was an <u>African American</u> born in the late 1800✗s to a society focused on segregating his people. However⊙ he knew very few boundaries in his life. He was able to get a college education, and he went on to be a grammar school principal. In 1897⊙ he became the first African American to pass the bar exam in Florida.

A few years later⊙ James and his brother together **wrote** the song "Lift Every Voice and Sing⊙" which eventually became the official anthem of the National Association for the Advancement of Colored People (or the NAACP). President Roosevelt appointed Johnson to diplomatic positions in Nicaragua and Venezuela.

In a society that largely saw African Americans as subpar⊙ James Johnson defied the odds and lived an **extraordinary** life.

Lesson 35

Lesson 35: Proofreading • Grammar

Spelling corrections are bold, and punctuation marks are circled.

The discovery of gold in California in 1848 changed the scope of many people⊙s **lives**. Thousands migrated west, dreaming of the wealth that **waited** beyond the horizon. Unfortunately, many dreamers lost everything. The cost of the supplies and the journey west squelched many dream⊗ before they really got started. Many even lost **their** lives chasing the riches.

Answer the following questions by selecting your choice from the answers given.

Which of the following sentences is an interrogative sentence?

a. I'm not sure what you're asking. b. Please clarify your question.

(c.) Are you hungry? d. I guess it's time for lunch.

What is the complete subject of this sentence? *Mary's teacher praised her efforts.*

(a.) Mary's teacher b. Mary c. praised d. praised her efforts

What is the complete predicate of the same sentence?

a. Mary's teacher b. Mary c. praised **(d.) praised her efforts**

Choose the simple subject and simple predicate of the same sentence.

a. Mary/efforts **(b.) teacher/praised** c. her/efforts

Lesson 43

Lesson 43: Parts of Speech

Which part of speech is each of the listed words? Write your choice on the line beside each word.

quickly __adverb__	curly __adjective__
running __verb__	them __pronoun__
thick __adjective__	very __adverb__
horse __noun__	was __verb__
among __preposition__	inch __noun__
us __pronoun__	long __adjective__
basket __noun__	often __adverb__
it __pronoun__	green __adjective__
is __verb__	beside __preposition__
myself __pronoun__	El Paso __noun__
tomorrow __adverb__	lovely __adjective__
under __preposition__	prance __verb__

Lesson 44

Lesson 44: Parts of Speech

Write the part of speech for the underlined word in each sentence.

The <u>hockey</u> puck flipped over the goal line. __adjective__

Will you join me on a morning <u>run</u>? __noun__

That taco salad <u>looks</u> delicious. __verb__

Have you <u>ever</u> had raw sushi? __adverb__

The cat is <u>beneath</u> the coffee table. __preposition__

Why don't you grab a <u>quick</u> snack? __adjective__

The dishes won't be washing <u>themselves</u>. __pronoun__

I can't <u>wait</u> for summer vacation. __verb__

Look <u>out</u> the window at that rainbow! __preposition__

The big <u>drink</u> spilled all over the van. __noun__

This store is in such a <u>remote</u> place. __adjective__

You need a <u>haircut</u>. __noun__

We should leave <u>soon</u> to get there on time. __adverb__

Lesson 46

Lesson 46: Possessives • Plurals

Choose the correct form of the possessive for each sentence.

The _____ toys were scattered all over the house.

childrens' **(children's)** childrens's

_____ glasses fell. Louis couldn't find them.

(Louis') Louis's Loui's

All of the _____ voices rose in harmony.

peoples' peoples's **(people's)**

The dog kept chasing _____ tail.

it's **(its)**

The one _____ hair is longer than the hair of the other two ____.

girl's/girls' girls'/girl's **(girl's/girls)**

Fill in the plurals of the words below.

bus __buses__	mosquito __mosquitoes__
roof __roofs__	deer __deer__
shelf __shelves__	cheek __cheeks__
batch __batches__	mix __mixes__

Lesson 47

Spelling corrections are bold, punctuation marks are circled, and capitalization errors are underlined.

Hedy Lamarr was an incredibly popular actress in the 1930's and 1940's. She had **roles** opposite such popular stars as Clark Gable and Jimmy Stewart. Hedy was known as "The Most Beautiful Woman in Film" by her contemporaries.

However, Hedy Lamarr was also incredibly intelligent. In 1942, along with her composer friend George Antheil, Hedy patented what she called the "Secret Communication System." It was originally concocted to solve an issue in World War II where the Nazis were decoding messages and blocking signals from radio-controlled missiles. It involved changing radio frequencies so that enemies couldn't detect the messages in the first place. The later invention of the transistor catapulted Hedy's invention into practical space, and it is still used today in both military applications as well as **cell** phone **technologies**.

Lesson 48

Fix the errors you find in the following paragraph. There are five mistakes.

Annie Oakley was forced to learn how to trap and shoot as early as age **eight** in order to support her family due to the death of her father. She became a fantastic shot while supporting her family, and she went on to join Buffalo Bill's Wild West show. Annie became a world-renowned rifle sharpshooter, one of the best of all time. It is believed that she taught more than 15,000 **women** to shoot a gun.

Lesson 49

Spelling corrections are bold, punctuation marks are circled, and capitalization errors are underlined.

In the 1950's, the space race was hot, particularly between the United States and the Soviet Union. Each nation wanted to be the first one to do a certain thing in space. Some of the firsts were the first launch into space, first animal in space, first human in space, first human to orbit the earth, and others. When the Soviet Union started to get the lead in the race, the United States, in desperation, opened a project with one goal. They **wanted** to nuke the moon.

The precision was important. The whole point of **nuking** the moon was making it visible to people. They **planned** to aim for the edge of the visible side of the moon. That way the cloud from the explosion would be illuminated by the sun and visible far and wide. Ultimately, the project was abandoned **due** to concerns about contaminating space or the bomb detonating early and **endangering** the inhabitants of the earth.

Lesson 51

Fill in the puzzle with the words below from *The Call of the Wild*.

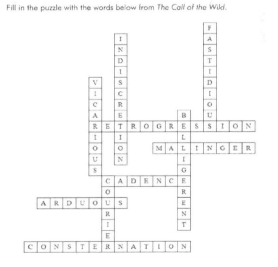

courier   consternation   arduous
malinger   cadence   retrogression
indiscretion   fastidious   vicarious
belligerent

.Lesson 52

Mark the part of speech for each word in the following sentence from *The Call of the Wild*: He took Buck by the scruff of the neck, and though the dog growled threateningly, dragged him to one side and replaced Sol-leks.

He	took	Buck	by
pronoun	verb	proper noun	preposition
the	scruff	of	the
article	noun	preposition	article
neck,	and	though	the
noun	conjunction	conjunction	article
dog	growled	threateningly,	dragged
noun	verb	adverb	verb
him	to	one	side
pronoun	preposition	adjective	noun
and		replaced	Sol-leks.
conjunction		verb	proper noun

Use this sentence to answer the following questions: *The general tone of the team picked up immediately.*

What's the simple subject of the sentence? **tone**

What's the complete subject? **the general tone of the team**

What's the predicate? **picked up immediately**

Lesson 53

Find the words from *The Call of the Wild* in the word search below.

morose	forevalued	deluged
remnant	solidarity	coveted
compelled	mates	floundered
convulsive	obdurate	lugubriously
	resiliency	

Lesson 54

Answer the questions about the sentence from *The Call of the Wild* below.

Thirty days from the time it left Dawson, the Salt Water Mail, with Buck and his mates at the fore, arrived in Skaguay.

What is the subject of the sentence? **the Salt Water Mail**

What is one prepositional phrase in the sentence? **from the time, at the fore, with Buck and his mates, at Skaguay**

Remember that **gerunds** are *ing* words that function as nouns. Write three sentences using gerunds.

(answers will vary)

Examples: Running is his favorite activity.

He also enjoys hiking.

He is afraid of flying.

Lesson 56

Play idiom hangman with someone! See if you can figure out these idioms in ten guesses or less. You might start with vowels or letters that are more common. Play with a sibling, parent, or friend to let you know if you're guessing correctly.

A B C D E F G H I J K L M N O P Q R S T U V W X Y Z

A penny for your thoughts

A B C D E F G H I J K L M N O P Q R S T U V W X Y Z

Barking up the wrong tree

A B C D E F G H I J K L M N O P Q R S T U V W X Y Z

Let sleeping dogs lie

A B C D E F G H I J K L M N O P Q R S T U V W X Y Z

Once in a blue moon

A B C D E F G H I J K L M N O P Q R S T U V W X Y Z

Don't give up your day job

A B C D E F G H I J K L M N O P Q R S T U V W X Y Z

It takes two to tango

Lesson 57

Lesson 57: Word Search
Language Arts 7

Find the words from *The Call of the Wild* in the word search below.

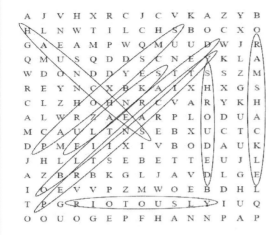

haunches   shrouded
paroxysms   pertinacity
obliterated   riotously
flanks   ramshackle

Lesson 58

Lesson 58: Gerunds
Language Arts 7

In each group of three, fill in the circle beside the sentence that contains the gerund. Underline it.

○ The rising smoke clouded the horizon.
● Much adventure can be found while <u>reading</u> books.
○ Smiling at them, she made her way into the room.

● <u>Blowing</u> bubbles in the yard is Ella's favorite activity.
○ Clara soaked in the tub to sooth her writhing muscles.
○ The tinkling ice made music in the glass.

○ Garret was blinded by all of the flashing cameras.
○ The speeding racecars were a blur.
● <u>Raising</u> children can be exhausting.

○ The twirling baton fell to the ground.
● <u>Killing</u> the bug made Andrew feel powerful.
○ Her growling stomach told her it was lunch time.

● <u>Eating</u> ice cream in the car can be messy.
○ Her hacking cough kept her up all night.
○ Natalie was enthralled by the flapping of the butterfly's wings.

○ Matthew was made dizzy by the spinning fan.
○ The leaping ballerinas were fun to watch.
● Caleb was excited about <u>baking</u> the cookies.

○ Giggling babies are the cutest.
○ The bouncing ball rolled down the hill
● <u>Singing</u> is Wyatt's favorite hobby.

Lesson 66

Lesson 66: Spelling - Crossword
Language Arts 7

Fill the words into the crossword puzzle using the letter clues and length of the words to help you.

calendar   mischievous
enthusiasm   mysterious
inconceivable   receive
inquiring   thief
interesting

Lesson 67

Lesson 67: Punctuation and Capitalization
Language Arts 7

Answer the following grammar questions.

An interrogative sentence ends with a __?__.

Is this sentence properly written? "Kate," said Mom, "please calm down."

a. yes   (b.) no (see corrections)

Apostrophes are used to show _____.

a. possession   b. missing letters   (c.) both

Circle the punctuation marks used incorrectly in this sentence. A lot of families have more than four children; for example, the Smith's, Johnson's, and Char's. (These are not possessive nouns.)

An imperative sentence would never end in a __?__.

Which of these sentences uses an apostrophe correctly?
a. The three girls' showed up late to class.
b. My dog's names are Dusty and Snickers.
(c.) Alabama's capital is Montgomery.
d. The church'es services let out early.

When you have a quotation inside of a quotation, you should use ____.
(a.) double quotes around single quotes   b. italics
c. commas

When you have a list of three or more items, you should use ____.
a. colons   b. conjunctions   (c.) commas

Which of these is *not* a proper use of a hyphen?
a. great-grandfather   (b.) thir-teen   c. thirty-three

Lesson 68

Lesson 68: Participle Phrases
Language Arts 7

In the following sentences, underline the participle phrases and circle what they are modifying.

Getting home on time, (she) raced inside.

Finishing the last lap, (he) raised his arms in victory.

Panting, (the dog) circled his bed and flopped down.

Glancing out the window, (they) noticed the rainbow.

Shooting the puck hard, (Matthew) scored a goal.

Saluting the flag, (the choir) sang the national anthem.

Gathering his things, (Braden) left for home.

Turning on his siren, (the police officer) chased the speeder.

In the following sentences, underline the gerund or the participle. On the line, write G if the underlined word is a gerund or P if it's a participle.

<u>Arriving</u> early is important to me.	G
<u>Whistling</u> while he worked, Daniel got the job done.	P
<u>Showing</u> his badge, the man was allowed to enter.	P
<u>Singing</u> is Sarah's favorite activity.	G
Eliana prefers <u>dancing</u>.	G
<u>Noticing</u> the deer in the road, Mom hit the brakes.	P
<u>Tripping</u> on his own two feet was Jake's specialty.	G
<u>Standing</u> tall, Jessica prepared to give her speech.	P

Lesson 71

Lesson 71: Nouns
Language Arts 7

Answer the following grammar questions.

The subject is who or what the sentence is about.

(a.) yes   b. no

Most nouns ending -y preceded by a vowel use -ies to make them plural.

a. yes   (b.) no

The preposition tells what happens in the sentence.

a. yes   (b.) no   (predicate)

Which noun is the subject of this sentence? *Most children from Toronto love playing hockey.*

(a.) children   b. Toronto   c. love   d. hockey

What is the predicate of this sentence? *Most children from Toronto love playing hockey.*

a. children   b. Toronto   (c.) love   d. hockey

Find the nouns in this sentence and tell whether they are singular or plural: *The girl's dresses were hanging in a row.*

(a.) singular, plural, singular   b. plural, plural, singular

Find the nouns in this sentence and tell whether they are singular or plural: *The men's beards were groomed with clippers.*

a. singular, plural, plural   (b.) plural, plural, plural

Which of these is punctuated correctly?

a. The childrens' game took all afternoon, amusing them thoroughly.

(b.) The crowd's cheers erupted at the quick, powerful pitch.

Lesson 76

Lesson 76: Spelling
Language Arts 7

Find the words from *The Spy* in the word search below.

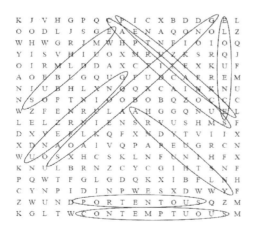

sublime	eloquence	portentous
ardently	petulance	contemptuous
unerring	capricious	soliloquizing

Lesson 77

Lesson 77: Proofreading
Language Arts 7

Spelling corrections are bold, punctuation marks are circled, and capitalization errors are underlined.

Famines can be caused by a lack of food or by a lack of access to food. There are many different causes of famines. Extreme **weather**, plant diseases, and animals can all cause a lack of food. Even **governments** can cut off access to food, resulting in famine.

Throughout history, weather has impacted our food supply. During horrible freezes or severe droughts, food prices in the United <u>States</u> and other civilized nations can skyrocket to compensate for the lack of crops. But in other areas of the world, weather causes true famine. Sometimes plants get diseases that cause them to die, creating the same lack of crops that weather can create. Animals and bugs can eat and destroy crops as well.

The most surprising cause of famine is tyrannical leaders who keep food from **their** own people. Today, many systems are in place to prevent governments from harming **their** own people in this way.

Lesson 78

Lesson 78: Proofreading

Spelling corrections are bold, punctuation marks are circled, and capitalization errors are underlined.

Manfred Albrecht Freiherr von Richthofen was a fighter pilot for <u>Germany</u> during World War 1. He became one of the most famous fighter pilots of **all** time throughout the course of the war. Painting his aircraft red **led** him to be called by the nicknames "Red Fighter Pilot," "Red Battle Flyer," and, most famously, "Red Baron."

The Red Baron was likely the deadliest fighter pilot in the entire war. He was officially credited with eighty air combat victories before his death. At one point during combat, a hit to the head caused him temporary blindness. He recovered well enough to successfully make a rough landing of his plane. Eventually, however, his reputation made him a very sought-after target. Everyone wanted credit for bringing down the Red Baron, and it's still unclear who ultimately put the permanent end to his combat career.

Lesson 79

Lesson 79: Proofreading

Spelling corrections are bold, punctuation marks are circled, and capitalization errors are underlined.

The city of Jerusalem is a fascinating place. Its historical background makes it a huge tourist location, drawing people from all parts of the world. But its biggest lure comes from its religious roots. In Hebrew, Yerushalayim means "foundation of peace." This name might be considered ironic. Since the city of Jerusalem is considered by three of the world's largest religions to be **their** religious center, it has been the reason for many wars over the centuries.

Christianity, Judaism, and Islam all consider Jerusalem to be important to **their** religion. Over the years, Jerusalem has seen the rise and fall of the kingdom of Israel, the death and resurrection of Jesus Christ, the Crusades, and many other so-called "holy wars." In fact, Israelis and Palestinians continue to fight over the **rights** to occupy Jerusalem **to** this day.

Lesson 86

Lesson 86: Spelling

Fill in the blanks with your spelling words. You can have someone read them to you from the answer key.

I would __**advise**__ against speaking disrespectfully.

What has been your greatest __**achievement**__ this year?

The sign said, "No __**admittance**__."

Can you offer your __**assistance**__ to that lady?

What's the postal __**abbreviation**__ for Massachusetts?

Do you submit to those in __**authority**__?

The sponge will __**absorb**__ the entire spill.

What's your __**advice**__ on this topic?

When I __**analyze**__ the budget, I see a deficit.

I have a close __**association**__ with my co-worker.

The state __**capitol**__ building is located downtown.

The infection in my throat was caused by __**bacteria**__.

Do you put __**cinnamon**__ on your applesauce?

The presidential __**campaign**__ was successful.

I rode my __**bicycle**__ to work yesterday.

What's all the __**commotion**__ outside?

The __**boulevard**__ winds its way by the beautiful park.

Lesson 87

Lesson 87: Parts of Speech • Brainstorming

Of the bolded words, circle the one that matches the part of speech to the side of the sentence.

The (swarming) gnats bothered my eyes. — Adjective

I guess I'll wash the dishes (myself.) — Pronoun

Let's go to the library (tomorrow.) — Adverb

The frog went for a (swim) in the pond. — Noun

That dog (looks) hungry. — Verb

My stomach growled loudly (during) the meeting. — Preposition

The (sweetly) scented lotion smelled like candy. — Adverb

Today (was) a very long day. — Verb

The top (of) the window **was covered** in dust. — Preposition

The (giggly) girls stayed up way too late. — Adjective

His (love) was boundless. — Noun

Is (that) your lost book? — Pronoun

Lesson 89

Day 89: Concrete and Abstract Nouns

For each noun, circle whether it is concrete or abstract.

jewelry box
(concrete) abstract

soccer ball
(concrete) abstract

book
(concrete) abstract

memory
concrete (abstract)

America
(concrete) abstract

magazine
(concrete) abstract

friendship
concrete (abstract)

bravery
concrete (abstract)

calendar
(concrete) abstract

pajamas
(concrete) abstract

championship
concrete (abstract)

lampshade
(concrete) abstract

talent
concrete (abstract)

Rebecca
(concrete) abstract

uniform
(concrete) abstract

future
concrete (abstract)

Lesson 90

Day 90: Plurals

For each noun, write the correct plural on the line.

yourself	yourselves	cherry	cherries
stimulus	stimuli	ellipsis	ellipses
deer	deer	mouse	mice
cactus	cacti	man	men
crutch	crutches	toy	toys
box	boxes	moose	moose
child	children	shelf	shelves
hero	heroes	pencil	pencils
tray	trays	potato	potatoes
latch	latches	baby	babies
sheep	sheep	calf	calves
bluff	bluffs	index	indices

Lesson 92

Lesson 92: Proofreading

Spelling corrections are bold, punctuation marks are circled, and capitalization errors are underlined.

Abigail Adams was the wife of the first <u>vice</u> <u>president</u> and second <u>president</u> of the United States⊙ John Adams. Though societal constraints of the day didn't allow Abigail to have any formal education⊙ she was self-educated and incredibly intelligent.

Abigail was a close confidant and advisor for her husband⊙ John. Many consider her to be one of the founders of the country because of the level of influence she had in his affairs. Historical letters written between the husband and wife show many intellectual discussions and are evidence of just how much John trusted his wife.

Abigail Adams believed in the importance of education⊙ and she home educated her five children. Her oldest son⊙ John Quincy Adams⊙ also went on to become <u>president</u>.

Lesson 93

Lesson 93: Proofreading

Rewrite the following paragraphs correctly. Be sure to proofread for errors in spelling, grammar, punctuation, capitalization, and usage.

Benjamin Franklin was a scientist inventor and writer. His most famous experiments dealt with electricity and he discovered many of it's governing laws. His work with electricity lead him to invent the lightening rod.

<u>Benjamin Franklin was a scientist⊙inventor⊙and writer. His</u> <u>most famous experiments **dealt** with electricity⊙and he</u> <u>discovered many of **its** governing laws. His work with</u> <u>electricity **led** him to invent the **lightning** rod.</u>

Franklin is considered won of americas Founding Fathers. He lived in england for many years as a representative of the colonist's who had gone to america. Though he never saw miliarty action during the revolutionary war, he did sign both the declaration of independance and the united states consitution.

<u>Franklin is considered **one** of **America's** Founding Fathers.</u> <u>He lived in **England** for many years as a representative of</u> <u>the **colonists** who had gone to **America**. Though he never</u> <u>saw **military** action during the **Revolutionary War**, he did</u> <u>sign both the **Declaration** of **Independence** and the</u> <u>United States Constitution.</u>

Lesson 94

Choose the correct pronoun to fill in the blank. If you need help, try to determine if the needed pronoun should be a subject or an object pronoun.

It was _____ who folded all of that laundry.

me   myself   **(I)**

My dad asked my brother and _____ to do our chores.

(me)   myself   I

Meg and _____ spent the entire day playing cards.

me   myself   **(I)**

My mom was not happy with _____ inviting several friends over without asking.

me   myself   **(my)**

Between you and _____, that dinner could have been a lot better.

(me)   myself   I

_____ spent all night on the phone together.

(She and Melanie)   Melanie and her

_____ friendship is important to me.

(Jennifer's and my) Me and Jennifer's   Myself and Jennifer's

Are you upset with _____ choosing of the movie?

me   myself   **(my)**

When it comes to haircuts, I like yours better than _____.

(mine)   mines   mine's

Lesson 95

Choose the correct pronoun to fill in the blank. If you need help, try to determine if the needed pronoun should be a subject or an object pronoun.

Are those glasses on the table _____ or mine?

(yours)   your's   yours'

Grandma requested that you call _____ and Aunt Carrie.

she   **(her)**

It was _____, that boy with the striped shirt, who threw the ball.

(he)   him

_____ wore heavy jackets on the ski trip.

Her and I   **(She and I)**   Her and me

It could have been _____ who left the flowers on the porch.

(he)   him

_____ share a locker.

(She and Becky)   Becky and her

Dad sat between _____ and Ashley so they wouldn't talk.

she   **(her)**

Ben realized that neither _____ nor Peter was ready for the exam.

(he)   him

Be sure to return to Mrs. Lovejoy what is _____.

(hers)   her's   hers'

Lesson 96

Answer the following questions by filling in the bubble beside your choice.

Which of these is a compound sentence?
- ● I'm really hungry, so I should stop for lunch.
- ○ I'm not sure where I left my shoes.
- ○ Do you know what Jessica's phone number is, or not?

Which of these is a complex sentence?
- ○ Mrs. Johnson took us to the library, and then she went to the store.
- ● When I grow up, I'm going to be a computer programmer.
- ○ We saw players, coaches, staff, and fans at the game.

Which of these is an independent clause?
- ○ If you have enough time
- ○ When I read books
- ● I don't want to get up

Which of these is correct?
- ○ "Come here," I said!
- ● "Come here!" I said.
- ○ "Come here." I said.

Her hair cascaded over her shoulders like a waterfall is an example of...
- ○ alliteration   ● simile   ○ metaphor

Weather and *whether* are...
- ○ synonyms   ○ antonyms   ● homophones

Love is war is an example of
- ○ alliteration   ○ simile   ● metaphor

Almost and *nearly* are...
- ● synonyms   ○ antonyms   ○ homophones

Lesson 97

Choose the correct pronoun to fill in the blank.

It was _____ who cleaned up the kitchen.

(we)   us

_____ whispering drew angry glances during the show.

Us   **(Our)**

That bag belongs to _____ two.

we   **(us)**

The teacher told _____ kids that we were really smart.

we   **(us)**

The car with the red flaking paint is _____.

(ours)   ours'   our's

We got all of the groceries in _____.

(ourselves)   ourself   ourself's

Match the topic with the best organization for it by writing the corresponding letter on the line.

A. research report   B. description
C. persuasive argument   D. instructions

How to make a peanut butter and jelly sandwich   __D__

Word picture of a sunset at the lake   __B__

Need for lower college tuition   __C__

Facts about internal combustion engines   __A__

Lesson 98

Choose the correct pronoun to fill in the blank.

The girls' kindness and _____ constant smiling warmed the hearts of the group leader.

(their)   them   they

_____ will be going to the diner if you'd like to join us.

(They and I)   I and them

Your seat is between _____.

Sammy and they   they and Sammy   (Sammy and them)

_____ and the other boys all loved to play basketball.

Their   Them   (They)

It was _____ who shoveled the snow off the deck.

their   them   (they)

When your brothers taunt you it's best to ignore _____ and their teasing.

their   (them)   they

Match the sentence to the type of writing by filling in the corresponding letter on the line.

A.   business report   B.   compare and contrast
C.   book review   D.   personal narrative

Vegetables are better for your health than fruit.   **B**

Charlotte's Web is a charming book about a spider.   **C**

The flat tire was just the beginning of my crazy day.   **D**

The Senate recently passed a controversial bill.   **A**

Lesson 99

Choose the correct pronoun to fill in the blank.

My friend is so calm; I wish I was as calm as _____.

her   (she)   herself

Jacob is a happy baby, and _____ giggling brightens a room.

him   (his)   himself

CJ is good at soccer, but I hope to be better than _____.

(he)   him   himself

_____ enjoyed our time at the fair.

Brandon and me   (Brandon and I)

The director commended _____ kids on our production.

(us)   we

I saw Alicia with that book, so I think it's _____.

her's   hers'   (hers)

They all saved up enough money _____.

theirselves   (themselves)   themselfs

Choose the more vivid word to complete the sentence.

The (tasty/(mouth-watering)) meal left us satisfied.

The ((exhausting)/hard) exercises strengthened my muscles.

My ((panting)/hot) dog needed a drink of water.

James was (mad/(indignant)) at the referee's call.

Lesson 100

Tell whether the following sentences have pronoun reference errors.

Sophia said Alaina raced her to the mailbox and she won.

(yes)   no

(It's not clear if "she" refers to Sophia or Alaina.)

It says in the newspaper that there is a big parade this weekend.

(yes)   no

("It" doesn't refer to anything. "The newspaper says that..." would be a better choice.)

Christy said that she needed to take a nap.

yes   (no)

("She" clearly refers to Christy.)

The girls used their crayons to make a big picture.

yes   (no)

("Their" refers to the girls.)

Lesson 103

Answer the questions about plurals by filling in the circle beside your choice.

The plural of "scenario" is...
○ scenarii   ● senarios   ○ scenarioes

The plural of "theory" is...
● theories   ○ theorys   ○ theory

The plural of "thief" is...
○ thiefs   ○ thief   ● thieves

The plural of "child" is...
○ childs   ● children   ○ childes

The plural of "root" is...
○ root   ○ rootes   ● roots

The plural of "curriculum" is...
● curricula   ○ curriculums   ○ curriculi

Spell the plural form of the word on the line beside it.

parenthesis   **parentheses**   berry   **berries**

mosquito   **mosquitoes**   fox   **foxes**

zero   **zeroes**   ox   **oxen**

stimulus   **stimuli**   goose   **geese**

Lesson 104

Fill in the circle beside the answer that best fits the blank.

This _____ meeting was a long one.
- ○ mornings
- ● morning's
- ○ mornings'

The top _____ brackets were failing.
- ● shelf's
- ○ shelves
- ○ shelfs'

The large assortment of _____ made my mouth water.
- ○ donut's
- ○ donuts'
- ● donuts

Our _____ belt was squeaking loudly.
- ○ vans
- ● van's
- ○ vans'

The three _____ lockers were all in a row.
- ○ boys
- ○ boy's
- ● boys'

I can hear that _____ cries from here!
- ● baby's
- ○ babys'
- ○ babies

The _____ purse was hanging off her shoulder.
- ○ women's
- ● woman's
- ○ womens'

I don't have all of my _____ in a row.
- ● ducks
- ○ duck's
- ○ ducks'

The _____ lids were bulging.
- ○ box's
- ○ box'es
- ● boxes'

We rode our _____ to the mall.
- ○ bikes'
- ● bikes
- ○ bike's

Lesson 105

Fill in the circle beside the answer that best fits the blank.

This _____ keyboard has sticky keys.
- ● computer's
- ○ computers'

The _____ restroom had a long line.
- ● women's
- ○ womens'

Those _____ reports took the entire day.
- ○ student's
- ● students'

The _____ message was deceiving.
- ● commercial's
- ○ commercials'

The three _____ ringers all went off at once.
- ○ phone's
- ● phones'

Those _____ stems are all missing.
- ○ cherry's
- ● cherries'

Are you wearing _____ jeans?
- ● men's
- ○ mens'

The _____ tails were all bushy.
- ○ fox's
- ● foxes'

That _____ cheese is oozing.
- ● sandwich's
- ○ sandwiches'

The _____ engine startled the entire neighborhood.
- ● motorcycle's
- ○ motorcycles'

Lesson 106

Study the word list in the Lesson Guide and then see how many words you can spell correctly when they are read to you. Learn from any mistakes you make.

admittance	analysis
artificial	attendance
biscuit	bizarre
boulevard	bouquet
bureau	campaign
cinnamon	commotion
confetti	culprit
deceive	democracy
embarrass	engineer

Lesson 107

Fill in the circle beside the statement that applies to the underlined word.

The Smith's invited the entire neighborhood to their pool party.
- ○ The word is correct.
- ● No apostrophe is necessary.

I wish you wouldn't eat your cookies on the couch.
- ● The word is correct.
- ○ No apostrophe is necessary.

The childrens' game was noisy.
- ○ The word is correct.
- ● The word should be children's.

Our two cities are meeting for the championship.
- ● The word is correct.
- ○ The word should be city's.

That blue house on the corner is our's.
- ○ The word is correct.
- ● No apostrophe is necessary.

That red house next to it is theirs'.
- ○ The word is correct.
- ● No apostrophe is necessary.

Jesse's notebook was left in our van.
- ● The word is correct.
- ○ No apostrophe is necessary.

The player's jerseys had a patch in support of cancer research.
- ○ The word is correct.
- ● The word should be players'.

Our friends' leg is in a cast.
- ○ The word is correct.
- ● The word should be friend's.

The tablet's screen has a crack in it.
- ● The word is correct.
- ○ No apostrophe is necessary.

Lesson 108

Lesson 108: Lose vs. Loose

Choose which word best fits the blank. Learn from any mistakes.

I don't want to _____ my glasses, but I need to take them off.
- ● lose
- ○ loose

Gather up your _____ change, and see if it's enough for a treat.
- ○ lose
- ● loose

The chain on my bike is _____.
- ○ lose
- ● loose

Even if we _____ the game, we still get a second place trophy.
- ● lose
- ○ loose

If we leave now, we'll _____ our place in line.
- ● lose
- ○ loose

My little brother has his first _____ tooth.
- ○ lose
- ● loose

I don't have any more baby teeth to _____.
- ● lose
- ○ loose

Don't win the battle, only to _____ the war.
- ● lose
- ○ loose

I always stretch to get _____ before a run.
- ○ lose
- ● loose

That _____ lug nut needs to be tightened on the hubcap.
- ○ lose
- ● loose

Lesson 109

Lesson 109: Who vs. Whom

Choose which word best fits the blank. Learn from any mistakes.

The waitress _____ you requested is off tonight.
- ○ who
- ● whom

He is the man _____ we met last week.
- ○ who
- ● whom

_____ brought me this beautiful bouquet?
- ● Who
- ○ Whom

_____ are you taking to the park with you?
- ○ Who
- ● Whom

I haven't yet decided _____ should get the main part.
- ● who
- ○ whom

She is the lady _____ we were looking for.
- ○ who
- ● whom

Wait until I tell you _____ I saw at the grocery store!
- ● who
- ○ whom

_____ should I say is asking?
- ● Who
- ○ Whom

_____ should we ask to dinner?
- ○ Who
- ● Whom

I need a helper on _____ I can depend.
- ○ who
- ● whom

Lesson 111

Day 111: Spellcheck

This paragraph contains five misspelled words. Can you figure out what they are and spell them correctly on the lines?

The United States House of Representatives is the lower chamber of the U.S. Congress. The Senate is the upper chamber. Together they make up the **legislachur** of the United States. The House of Representatives has a fixed number of 435 members, voted into office every **to** years. Each state gets a number of representatives in proportion to its population. The least populated states get only one representative, while the more **populus** states currently have over fifty. Representatives are spread around the state, **speeking** for different congressional districts that might have different needs or desires. The House votes on bills that have the **potenchul** to eventually become laws. The House of Representatives plays an important role in the checks and balances of the United States government.

legislature   two

populous   speaking

potential

Lesson 112

Lesson 112: Plurals and Possessives

Fill in the circle beside the answer that best fits the blank.

The _____ were intense.
- ● exercises
- ○ exercise's
- ○ exercises'

The _____ smile was a bit creepy.
- ○ skeletons
- ● skeleton's
- ○ skeletons'

Both of my _____ have flat tires.
- ● bikes
- ○ bike's
- ○ bikes'

The two _____ pictures complemented each other.
- ○ posters
- ○ poster's
- ● posters'

The _____ rungs were spaced twelve inches apart.
- ○ ladders
- ● ladder's
- ○ ladders'

That _____ incline was difficult to climb.
- ○ hills
- ● hill's
- ○ hills'

The three _____ heads popped up in unison.
- ○ squirrels
- ○ squirrel's
- ● squirrels'

Neither of the two _____ were working.
- ● microwaves
- ○ microwave's
- ○ microwaves'

That _____ numbers were faded.
- ○ keypads
- ● keypad's
- ○ keypads'

Those _____ roofs make an interesting skyline.
- ○ buildings
- ○ building's
- ● buildings'

Lesson 114

Lesson 114: Plurals and Possessives

Fill in the circle beside the answer that best fits the blank.

The _____ weave hurt my eyes.
- ○ carpets ● carpet's ○ carpets'

The two _____ antlers were locked together.
- ○ deers ● deer's ○ deers'

The _____ decision was to build the park.
- ○ peoples ● people's ○ peoples'

The area _____ are closed.
- ● schools ○ school's ○ schools'

The four _____ hands all showed different times.
- ○ clocks ○ clock's ● clocks'

The _____ angles made it difficult to paint.
- ○ ceilings ● ceiling's ○ ceilings'

All four _____ rolled down the hill faster than we could run.
- ● balls ○ ball's ○ balls'

The _____ drawings showcased her talent.
- ○ girls ● girl's ○ girls'

The two _____ laces didn't match.
- ○ shoes ○ shoe's ● shoes'

The _____ wouldn't work because the _____ were dead.
- ● flashlights/batteries ○ flashlight's/batteries ○ flashlights'/batteries'

Lesson 116

Lesson 116: Possessives

Choose the correct form of the possessive for each sentence.

_____ car was a bright shade of red.
- (Cindy's) Cindys' Cindies'

_____ car was a darker shade.
- Chris' (Chris's) Chri's

The _____ department is downstairs.
- mens mens' (men's)

The two _____ fins cut through the water towards us.
- shark's (sharks') sharks

The book landed on _____ spine.
- its' it's (its)

The seven _____ windows were left open in the rain.
- bus's (buses') buses's

Your shearers shaved a lot of _____ wool.
- (sheep's) sheeps' sheeps

My _____ names are Whisper and Mittens.
- cats (cats') cat's

The _____ feathers ruffled as it landed.
- (goose's) geeses' geese's

That _____ antenna is broken.
- radioes radios' (radio's)

Lesson 121

Lesson 121: Spelling

See how many words you can spell correctly the first time as they are read to you. Learn from any mistakes you make.

fabricate	fascinating
flagrant	foreign
forfeit	frequently
genuine	gossiping
grammar	grievance
guarantee	harass
havoc	heroic
horrify	hospital
humid	hygiene

Lesson 122

Lesson 122: Spelling - Unscramble

Unscramble your spelling words.

AABTFEICR	fabricate
THPILOSA	hospital
CVNEGERIA	grievance
NRIGEOF	foreign
OIRYHFR	horrify
UIMDH	humid
RNUGETAAE	guarantee
RFNALATG	flagrant
CHVAO	havoc
INATINFGCSA	fascinating
SOPGNSGII	gossiping
NEYHEGI	hygiene
IOCREH	heroic
IFEORTF	forfeit
INEUGNE	genuine
SSAAHR	harass
AMGARRM	grammar
FULYEQNTRE	frequently

Lesson 123

Fill in the blanks with the correct spelling word. Be sure to spell it correctly!

There is no __guarantee__ that you will win.

Did you just __harass__ that officer?

It would __horrify__ Mother to know what you said.

Don't __fabricate__ a story to stay out of trouble.

The history museum is __fascinating__ to me.

Are we going to finish our game or do you __forfeit__?

It is so __humid__ outside this summer.

The rain is wreaking __havoc__ on my hair.

Grandpa is being released from the __hospital__ today.

Snow is a __foreign__ concept to warmer climates.

The __flagrant__ foul cost the team the game.

It snows __frequently__ in many northern states.

Her __heroic__ act saved the puppy from being trapped.

The neighbor filed a __grievance__ about the loud party.

The girls were caught __gossiping__ about their teacher.

The boy's kindness was __genuine__.

Always check spelling and __grammar__ in your papers.

Her __hygiene__ habits were pristine.

Lesson 124

Play hangman! See if you can figure out your spelling words in ten guesses or less. Cross out letters you've guessed to help yourself keep track. The words are in the Lesson Guide.

A B C D E F G H I J K L M N O P Q R S T U V W X Y Z

f o r f e i t

A B C D E F G H I J K L M N O P Q R S T U V W X Y Z

h e r o i c

A B C D E F G H I J K L M N O P Q R S T U V W X Y Z

h a r a s s

A B C D E F G H I J K L M N O P Q R S T U V W X Y Z

h o r r i f y

A B C D E F G H I J K L M N O P Q R S T U V W X Y Z

h u m i d

A B C D E F G H I J K L M N O P Q R S T U V W X Y Z

g r a m m a r

Lesson 125

See how many words you can spell correctly now as they are read to you. Learn from any mistakes you make.

fabricate	fascinating
flagrant	foreign
forfeit	frequently
genuine	gossiping
grammar	grievance
guarantee	harass
havoc	heroic
horrify	hospital
humid	hygiene

Lesson 126

See how many words you can spell correctly the first time as they are read to you. Learn from any mistakes you make.

identical	idle
idol	immediately
immobilize	impossibility
inconvenient	incredible
infamous	innocence
instructor	intelligent
irate	irresistible
judgment	juvenile
kettle	knitting

Lesson 127

Unscramble your spelling words.

ITNTIKGN	knitting
LIACNDETI	identical
NSIFMUOA	infamous
EYTALIIMMDE	immediately
NTLELIETNGI	intelligent
NBRLEDCEII	incredible
ELETTK	kettle
DOLI	idol
CIONENNCE	innocence
NELIVEJU	juvenile
ILOMIEZMBI	immobilize
TSIIRERBESLI	irresistible
DNGTJUEM	judgment
TPLIYSOMSIBII	impossibility
CTNUSRORTI	instructor
NNCNEOVTIEIN	inconvenient
IEART	irate
LDIE	idle

Lesson 128

Fill in the blanks with the correct spelling word. Be sure to spell it correctly!

My dance __instructor__ taught us ballet.

Your mother is __knitting__ a beautiful blanket.

The __infamous__ robber was caught red-handed.

__Idle__ hands lead to trouble.

My sister was __irate__ when I read her diary.

The tea __kettle__ is whistling on the stove.

These cookies are absolutely __irresistible__.

Declaring his __innocence__, the man walked away.

Stop blowing bubbles in your milk. It's so __juvenile__!

What an __incredible__ sunset.

This detour is very __inconvenient__.

Many people treat money as an __idol__.

We had to __immobilize__ his leg after he landed on it.

Do you know any __identical__ twins?

I need you to come here __immediately__!

Use your best __judgment__ when choosing.

The boy is so __intelligent__ he taught the teacher.

Finishing schoolwork can seem like an __impossibility__.

Lesson 129

Play hangman! See if you can figure out your spelling words in ten guesses or less. Cross out letters you've guessed to help yourself keep track. The words are in the Lesson Guide.

A B C D E F G H I J K L M N O P Q R S T U V W X Y Z

j u d g m e n t

A B C D E F G H I J K L M N O P Q R S T U V W X Y Z

k e t t l e

A B C D E F G H I J K L M N O P Q R S T U V W X Y Z

i d l e .

A B C D E F G H I J K L M N O P Q R S T U V W X Y Z

i n f a m o u s

A B C D E F G H I J K L M N O P Q R S T U V W X Y Z

i r a t e .

A B C D E F G H I J K L M N O P Q R S T U V W X Y Z

j u v e n i l e

Lesson 130

See how many words you can spell correctly the first time as they are read to you. Learn from any mistakes you make.

identical	idle
idol	immediately
immobilize	impossibility
inconvenient	incredible
infamous	innocence
instructor	intelligent
irate	irresistible
judgment	juvenile
kettle	knitting

Lesson 131

Lesson 131: Infinitives
Language Arts 7

Find and underline all of the infinitives in the following story.

We want **to go** to the park this afternoon. It's going **to be** a nice, sunny day. The temperature is hovering right around 70 degrees, a perfect day **to swing** in the breeze.

We're planning **to take** a picnic with us. My sister is going **to eat** a sandwich, but my brother prefers **to have** fruit salad. I think the fruit salad is just going **to attract** ants and bees, so I'll be sure **to use** bug spray before we head out to the park.

My favorite thing **to do** at the park is kick the ball around with my siblings. Hopefully this time my brother doesn't accidentally hit my sister in the face with the ball. No one needs **to hear** her shriek like that again! But I need **to remind** my brother **to take** some allergy medicine before we leave. Otherwise, he's going **to sneeze** for the rest of the day!

Lesson 132

Lesson 132: Spelling
Language Arts 7

Find the words from *The Talisman* in the word search below.

```
K  L  D  I  Z  U  I  N  C  O  N  I  J  Y  T
O  A  A  Q  M  Z  A  T  I  R  O  L  W  N  V
I  U  H  X  U  I  E  U  K  S  Y  O  U  Q  R
L  R  P  Z  N  V  T  T  H  E  W  I  P  N  P
S  E  O  U  Y  Z  I  I  E  Z  T  W  Q  O  C
F  L  Y  H  C  C  W  O  G  A  R  Q  R  P  E
P  S  I  X  A  B  J  Y  C  A  D  L  L  L  U
J  Q  S  L  B  R  I  I  B  I  L  C  Y  I
P  S  D  C  B  E  F  I  D  R  W  I  W  A  C
T  F  D  G  B  I  R  O  E  J  K  O  W  V
J  B  R  E  T  K  O  N  O  D  I  Z  N  R
L  Q  I  R  Q  S  K  I  M  Z  A  B  O  X  F
D  U  Q  B  Y  Q  S  E  J  L  W  O  A  C  J
G  M  T  N  E  A  U  D  A  C  I  O  U  S  U
P  Y  L  S  M  F  S  U  J  B  Q  G  T  P  F
```

audacious   laurels   mitigation

mortification   sinewy   sordid

taciturn

Lesson 133

Lesson 133: Spelling
Language Arts 7

Fill in the blanks with your spelling words. You can have someone read them to you from the answer key.

The park included three **acres** of luscious grass.

The seatbelt was **adjustable** to fit her small waist.

The **afghan** kept her warm when the heat went out.

What's your **analysis** of this situation?

This **artificial** sweetener has an aftertaste.

Are you **absolutely** certain you turned off the stove?

What has been your greatest **achievement** this year?

Iris picked a lovely **bouquet** of wildflowers.

Congratulations are in order for the winners.

The crowd threw **confetti** as the newlyweds ran past.

The **capital** of California is Sacramento.

Chase likes to put honey on his morning **biscuit**.

Sara put her jewelry box on top of the **bureau**.

It seems a mouse was the cookie thief **culprit**.

The **competition** was fierce at the spelling bee.

Not to **embarrass** you, but there's lettuce in your teeth.

The item's **description** said it was brand new.

The project **engineer** said the build was on schedule.

Lesson 134

Lesson 134: Gerunds and Infinitives
Language Arts 7

Does the sentence need a gerund or an infinitive? Write the proper form of the word in parentheses on the line in the sentence, and then tell whether it is a gerund (g) or infinitive (i) on the line at the end.

Are you free **to work** this weekend? — **i**
(work)

I expect you **to clean** up that spill. — **i**
(clean)

I don't mind **reading** to you while you clean. — **g**
(read)

Can you tell me how **to get** to the library? — **i**
(get)

I can't picture Todd **dancing** to the music. — **g**
(dance)

The girls are **jumping** on the trampoline. — **g**
(jump)

Do you plan **to go** to the park? — **i**
(go)

Consider **researching** Lincoln for your paper. — **g**
(research)

Are you **running** the marathon this weekend? — **g**
(run)

We chose **to walk** the 5K. — **i**
(walk)

Lesson 137

Lesson 137: Dangling modifiers
Language Arts 7

Each of the sentences below contains a dangling modifier. Rewrite each sentence so that the participle phrase modifies the noun it should.

(Answers will vary, suggestions given)

Covered in delicious, sugary syrup, mother served the towering pile of pancakes.

Mother served the towering pile of pancakes that were covered in delicious, sugary syrup.

Soaked to the bone, everything Haylee touched became wet as well.

Since Haylee was soaked to the bone, everything she touched became wet as well.

Running all day and night, we called a handyman to fix the heater.

We called a handyman to fix the heater that was running all day and night.

Lesson 138

Lesson 138: Dangling modifiers
Language Arts 7

Choose the sentence of each group that is formatted correctly by filling in the circle next to your choice.

○ Straining to see the stage, the seats were too far back for my nearsighted sister.

● The seats were too far back for my nearsighted sister, who was straining to see the stage.

○ The seats, too far back for my nearsighted sister, were straining to see the stage.

○ Sweetly smiling, the bouquet was received by my mother.

○ The bouquet was received by my mother, sweetly smiling.

● Sweetly smiling, my mother received the bouquet.

● Kicking the ball, my brother broke the kitchen window.

○ Kicking the ball, the kitchen window was broken by my brother.

○ Breaking the kitchen window, the ball was kicked by my brother.

○ Sitting down to dinner, the wonderful aroma made us all drool.

○ The wonderful aroma, sitting down to dinner, made us all drool.

● We all drooled at the wonderful aroma as we sat down to dinner.

Lesson 139

Lesson 139: Dangling modifiers
Language Arts 7

Underline each sentence in the following story that has a dangling or misplaced modifier.

Last weekend, my family went on a camping trip. _Arriving at our destination early, the campsite wasn't ready yet._ Deciding to go for a walk, we hiked around the campground to get the lay of the land. We figured it'd be nice to know what to expect from our weekend. _Spotting a creek, my camera wouldn't focus well enough to get a picture of the meandering water._ _Swallowing my disappointment, my dad called me over to check out the pool._ Noticing the slide, I perked up a little. I love a good pool slide.

At long last, we got the text that our campsite was ready. _Setting up our tent, the dog started barking. Following his gaze, the park ranger was seen coming up to our site._ Informing us of an issue with the site we were on, the ranger offered a free upgrade to a fully loaded camper. Needless to say, we had a fabulous weekend roughing it in the woods!

Lesson 141

Lesson 141: Spellcheck
Language Arts 7

This paragraph contains five misspelled words. Can you figure out what they are and spell them correctly on the lines?

When the original American colonists decided to revolt against British rule, there were many who were convinced the endeavor was destined for failure. Of course, without the benefit of hindsight, that feels like a fair assessment. After all, the colonists had an enormous undertaking to **acomplish**. They were attempting to **addopt** an entirely original form of government. They needed to **addhere** to a whole new **adsortment** of laws and legislations. While modern American leaders might **agravate** the world from time to time, the fledgling band of revolutionaries that started the United States achieved an incredible feat.

accomplish	_adopt_
adhere	_assortment_
aggravate	

Lesson 142

Based on this excerpt, Tom must be...
- ○ The prince
- ● The pauper
- ○ Neither

According to the third paragraph, Tom's dreams made his reality...
- ○ sweeter
- ○ like a dream
- ● even more horrible
- ○ intense

We get the idea in this excerpt that Tom is...
- ● a poor beggar child
- ○ happy with his childhood
- ○ lonely
- ○ a good student

Read this line from the first paragraph: *he tramped despondently up and down the region* – in which of these words does the suffix –ly mean the same as it does in the word *despondently*?
- ○ curly
- ○ melancholy
- ● giggly
- ○ fly

Tom was kept awake by...
- ○ fighting
- ○ hunger
- ○ pain
- ● all of these

Lesson 143

Reread the excerpt from Mark Twain's *The Prince and the Pauper* in lesson 142 and then answer the questions.

Tom's father and grandmother were...
- ○ uncaring
- ○ happy that Tom was forlorn
- ○ beggars
- ● moved by his tired, wet condition

Based on the context, *"dreadful pork-pies and other deadly inventions"* was describing food Tom believed to be...
- ○ poisoned
- ○ disgusting
- ● delicious
- ○ too expensive

A good description of the weather in the excerpt would be...
- ○ cheerful
- ● glum
- ○ nervous
- ○ indifferent

The word *execute* at the end of the first paragraph means...
- ○ kill
- ● carry out
- ○ write down
- ○ hang

According to the third paragraph, a good synonym for Tom's surroundings would be...
- ● disgusting
- ○ pleasant
- ○ congenial
- ○ boring

Lesson 144

Reread the excerpt from Mark Twain's *The Prince and the Pauper* in lesson 142 and then answer the questions.

That Tom *"fell asleep in the company of jewelled and gilded princelings"* means that he...
- ○ really was rich and just pretended to be poor
- ○ was sleeping somewhere other than his home
- ● was dreaming
- ○ was a prince

Which of these words from the story uses a suffix to change an adjective into a noun?
- ● wretchedness
- ○ murky
- ○ delicious
- ○ princelings

According to the excerpt, Tom's dream of being a prince was...
- ○ the first one he'd had
- ○ unusual
- ● a normal occurrence
- ○ we don't have information about it

Judging from the context, a good synonym for the word "obeisance" would be...
- ○ annoyance
- ○ ignorant
- ○ intelligence
- ● respect

Why was Tom in tears at the end of the excerpt?
- ○ He was poor.
- ○ He wished to be a prince.
- ○ His dream had made his reality seem that much worse.
- ● all of the above

Lesson 145

The first sentence of the excerpt, *"This was very uncomfortable, and I was half afraid,"* is a _____ sentence.
- ○ simple
- ● compound
- ○ complex

Which of these words from the excerpt has a prefix that means "not"?
- ○ entered
- ○ arranged
- ● unknown
- ○ materials

Which of these words from the excerpt has a suffix that means "most"?
- ○ dependent
- ○ dressing
- ○ confusedly
- ● strangest

Which word describes the room in which the narrator finds himself in this scene?
- ○ comfortable
- ● chaotic
- ○ tidy
- ○ dark

The woman in the scene appears to be...
- ● rich
- ○ dirty
- ○ mute
- ○ young

Lesson 146

Lesson 146: Reading Comprehension

Reread the excerpt from Charles Dickens' *Great Expectations* in lesson 145 and then answer the questions.

Based on the description given, it would seem the woman in this scene was a...
- ● bride
- ○ fashion designer
- ○ beggar
- ○ we don't know

What does the narrator imply was his biggest clue that the prominent table in the room was "*a fine lady's dressing-table*"?
- ○ the gilded looking-glass
- ○ that it was a draped table
- ● the fine lady sitting at it
- ○ the bright jewels

Which of these best portrays how the woman is likely feeling, given the described scene?
- ○ happy
- ○ energized
- ○ organized
- ● sad

The narrator describes himself as...
- ● uncomfortable
- ○ confident
- ○ timid
- ○ young

The narrator describes the woman as...
- ○ put together
- ○ boisterous
- ● strange
- ○ messy

Lesson 147

Lesson 147: Reading Comprehension

Reread the excerpt from Charles Dickens' *Great Expectations* on day 145 and then answer the questions.

All of the sentences in this excerpt are which type of sentence?
- ● declarative
- ○ interrogative
- ○ exclamatory
- ○ imperative

Why did the woman only have one shoe on?
- ● she hadn't put the other on yet (or had taken it off already)
- ○ she couldn't find the other shoe
- ○ she only had one leg
- ○ we don't know

Reread this line from the first paragraph: *This was very uncomfortable, and I was half afraid.* In which of these words does the suffix –able mean the same as it does in the word *uncomfortable*?
- ○ table
- ○ cable
- ● doable
- ○ fable

A majority of this excerpt is which part of a story?
- ○ character development
- ● a description of setting
- ○ plot
- ○ climax

What explanation of the scene would make sense given the information we have?
- ○ there was an earthquake
- ● the woman's fiancé left her at the altar
- ○ the narrator was a robber
- ○ the electricity was out

Lesson 148

Lesson 148: Reading Comprehension

The likely setting for this story, based on this passage, is...
- ● an orphanage
- ○ a hospital
- ○ a police station
- ○ a library

What is the problem the boys are facing in this excerpt?
- ○ they're overworked
- ○ they're tired
- ● they're hungry
- ○ they don't like the master

Which of these words from the excerpt has a suffix that means "full of"?
- ○ generally
- ● voracious
- ○ companions
- ○ reckless

Read this part of a sentence from the excerpt: *...the boy who slept next him, who happened to be a weakly youth of tender age.* The word *weakly* here is being used as a(n)...
- ○ noun
- ○ verb
- ● adjective
- ○ adverb

The master was _____ Oliver's request.
- ○ pleased with
- ○ understanding of
- ○ depressed because of
- ● furious about

Lesson 149

Lesson 149: Reading Comprehension

Reread the excerpt from Charles Dickens' *Oliver Twist* in lesson 148 and then answer these questions.

Reread this partial sentence from the excerpt: *He rose from the table; and advancing to the master, basin and spoon in hand, said: somewhat alarmed at his own temerity: "Please, sir, I want some more."* Based on the context, a good synonym for *temerity* would be...
- ○ timidity
- ● boldness
- ○ stupidity
- ○ friendliness

Does it seem that the assistants had ever heard an orphan ask for seconds?
- ○ yes
- ● no

In this excerpt, what is *gruel*?
- ● food
- ○ work
- ○ exhaustion
- ○ anger

Which of these words from the excerpt is a compound word?
- ○ hunger
- ○ pinioned
- ○ desperate
- ● somewhat

True or false: Oliver came empty-handed for seconds.
- ○ true
- ● false

Lesson 150

Reread the excerpt from Charles Dickens' *Oliver Twist* in lesson 148 and then answer these questions.

Which of these words from the excerpt has a suffix that means "characterized by"?
- ○ stupefied
- ○ paralysed
- ● healthy
- ○ reckless

The excerpt explicitly states that the master was...
- ○ mean
- ● fat
- ○ angry
- ○ hungry

What conflict is the main catalyst for the climax of this excerpt?
- ● the boys are hungry
- ○ the master is mean

Read this sentence from the first paragraph: *Boys have generally excellent appetites.* – in which of these words does the suffix –ent mean the same as it does in the word *excellent*?
- ○ accent
- ○ percent
- ○ agent
- ● absorbent

Did Oliver get his seconds?
- ○ yes
- ● no

Lesson 151

This paragraph contains five misspelled words. Can you figure out what they are and spell them correctly on the lines?

Many scientists believe the world to be millions, if not billions, of years old. Various scientific publications **repetedly** state this as fact. However, there are a growing number of scientists who now believe the earth to be much younger than previously thought. Several dating methods have been proven to be inaccurate. Sometimes in science, the best we can do is **speculait**. Our speculations can **coincied** with available data, but no one can **guarantie** that their way is right. **Altho** some parts of our physical universe can be proven, many continue to be a mystery.

repeatedly   speculate

coincide   guarantee

although

Lesson 153

As a reminder, a **simple sentence** is simple – just one subject and predicate combination. *This is an example of a simple sentence.*

A **compound sentence** takes two simple sentences and compounds them, squashes them together using something like——"and", "or", "but"——in the middle to connect them. *This is an example of a compound sentence, and I have made it with two simple sentences joined together into one.*

A **complex sentence** takes a simple sentence and adds another subject and predicate in a way that they don't form another sentence on their own. *This is an example of a complex sentence because I have added a second subject and verb in a way that can't stand on its own.*

Identify these sentence types (from ch. 3 of *The King Will Make a Way*). The answers are simple, compound, or complex.

He crouched and examined mushrooms, pine cones, rocks and beetles.

simple

Gabe kept up the maneuvers until the guard was safely settled back in his guard box, comfortably seated on his stool.

complex

The toad hopped off just beyond him, and the natural impulse of a ten-year-old boy to try and catch it overpowered him.

compound

He looked up and his heart melted.

compound

Unthinking, he flung himself at the King's feet.

simple

Even though the hill was just a few stone throws away from the inn, he felt like a pioneer——adventurous and alone.

complex

Lesson 156

As a reminder, there are four types of sentences: declarative, interrogative, exclamatory, and imperative.

Declarative sentences make statements. *Today is my birthday.*

Interrogative sentences ask questions. *Is today your birthday?*

Exclamatory sentences exclaim. *Today is my birthday!*

Imperative sentences command. *Today's your birthday, so celebrate!*

Identify the sentence types of the sentences from chapter 5 of *The King Will Make a Way*.

Sentence	Type
He sat up straighter.	declarative
When is it coming?	interrogative
Relax.	imperative
What are you saying?	interrogative
Father was worried.	declarative
Yes, sir!	exclamatory
Get inside and stay there!	imperative/exclamatory
This is going to be a bad storm!	exclamatory
Tabitha shrieked.	declarative
Remember the old village song?	interrogative

Lesson 163

Lesson 163: Dialogue
Language Arts 7

Properly punctuate the dialogue at the top of the page. Then use the lines at the bottom of the page to copy the interesting quote by your historical person.

"Come here," he said.

She got up and crossed the room. "What is it?"

"A geode."

She asked again, "And that is what exactly?"

He brought out a hammer. "Watch and see."

_____
_____
_____
_____
_____
_____
_____
_____

Lesson 164

Lesson 164: Uncommon Punctuation
Language Arts 7

Add the missing punctuation to this sentence. Be sure to include any uncommon punctuation (semicolon, colon, dash).

I had too much on my mind, so I got out of bed to make myself a list of what I needed to do: call mom, Jenny, and the plumber; bake the cookies; take pictures of the kids; and update the blog—just so I could get some sleep!

Write a sentence or a paragraph that uses a semicolon, a colon, and a dash.

_____
_____
_____
_____
_____
_____
_____
_____

Lesson 166

Lesson 166: Anthropomorphism
Language Arts 7

Anthropomorphism is a literary device where something non-human becomes humanlike in form and/or behavior. Read this sentence from chapter 15 of *The King Will Make a Way*:

Despair circled Gabe like a vulture, taunting, laughing. "He's dead. He's dead. They're all dead. Lifeless bodies left for the birds. You might as well join them. Vulpine will be after you next."

What nonliving thing is taking on human attributes? **despair**

What human qualities did it have? **taunting, laughing, speaking**

Now you try it. Look at the pen or pencil in your hand. Make it come alive. What is it thinking as you are holding it, writing with it? What would it say when you are chewing on it, tapping it? Give it a personality and write a little story with the pen or pencil as the main character. Give his point of view on the world.

_____
_____
_____
_____
_____
_____
_____
_____

Lesson 167

Lesson 167: Lie vs. Lay
Language Arts 7

In the present tense, lie is what you do to yourself, and lay is what you do to something else. Fill in these blanks with lie or lay:

I **lie** on my bed to rest.

A chicken **lay**s an egg.

In the past tense, lie becomes lay, and lay becomes laid. Fill in these blanks with lie, lay, or laid:

I want to **lie** down for a nap.

Last week I **laid** out the pattern for the dress.

I need to **lay** out the schedule for everyone to see.

He **lay** there for hours yesterday.

See if you can figure out the correct word for each blank.

My cat is _____ in the light.
○ laying ● lying

She often _____ there.
● lies ○ lays

I _____ my toothbrush on the sink.
○ lay ● laid

The US _____ to the north of Mexico.
● lies ○ lays

We hope you had a great year with EP Language Arts 7.

EP provides free, complete, high quality online homeschool curriculum for children around the world. Find more of our courses and resources on our site, allinonehomeschool.com.

If you prefer offline materials, consider Genesis Curriculum which takes a book of the Bible and turns it into daily lessons in science, social studies, and language arts for your children to learn all together. The curriculum also includes learning Biblical languages. Genesis Curriculum offers Rainbow Readers and A Mind for Math, a math curriculum designed for about first through fourth grade to be done all together. Each math lesson is based on the day's Bible reading from the main curriculum. GC Steps is an offline preschool and kindergarten program. Learn more about our curriculum on our site, GenesisCurriculum.com.

Made in the USA
Coppell, TX
26 July 2023

19618539R00044